Praise for *The Domino Theory*

"Ed Capozzi found an ingenious way to drain the verbal swamp of proximate cause and make the concept as clear and easy for the jury as a row of falling dominos. The proof of its merit is that it seems so obvious in hindsight. I said to myself, 'Why didn't I think of that?'— the mark of a really good idea."

— Patrick Malone, member of the Inner Circle of Advocates, coauthor of *Rules of the Road*, author of *The Fearless Cross-Examiner*

"An engaging book about proximate cause. With *The Domino Theory*, Ed Capozzi gives you tips and insight on how to come up with bold strategies for demonstrating this confusing jury issue."

— Rodney Jew, litigation strategist

"Too many well-tried plaintiff's cases have been lost because of juror confusion over what proximate cause means. With brilliant simplicity, Ed Capozzi presents an intuitive and logical approach that allows jurors to hear and see how the accident cause connects to the injury evidence, enabling them to 'get it.'

And the book is something far more than that. It is a plaintiff lawyer's roadmap to success. Ed takes the reader through a methodology that, if followed faithfully, will bring success beyond imagination. I have been trying personal injury cases for forty-two years, and Ed brings a rarely encountered wisdom to so-called 'garden variety' soft-tissue cases. Once you adopt and practice the domino theory, you will never ever call a soft-tissue case 'garden variety' again, and nor will your adversaries."

— Michael Maggiano, past president of the New Jersey Association for Justice and the Melvin Belli Society, member of the Million Advocates Dollar Forum, and fellow of the American College of Trial Lawyers

"Ed Capozzi's *The Domino Theory* is the ultimate set of builders' plans and specifications on how to prevail on the most vital issues in every personal injury case. It is a masterpiece of winning advocacy. This book will help every plaintiff's attorney maximize the result for his or her client. It is such a fun and interesting read. Every~~~~~~

D1522667

firm will have this book—it is a practitioner's manual on how to get it done! Ed's writing makes for such a practical and easy-to-understand guidebook on practices, steps, principles, and more. The chapter-by-chapter "Takeaways" are stepping stones to victory. This book is a must for every trial lawyer's library!"

—John Romano, past president of the Academy of Florida Trial Lawyers, the Southern Trial Lawyers Association, and the National Trial Lawyers Association

The
Domino Theory

Edward P. Capozzi

Trial Guides, LLC

Trial Guides, LLC, Portland, Oregon 97210

ISBN: 978-1-941007-43-3

Library of Congress Control Number: 2016938337

Trial Guides, LLC

Attn: Permissions

2350 NW York Street

Portland, OR 97210

(800) 309-6845

www.trialguides.com

Editor: Travis Kremer

Proofreader: Jacoba Lawson

Cover Designers: Miroslava Sobot & Michael Fofrich

Interior Template Designer: Laura Lind Design

Printed and bound in the United States of America.

Printed on acid-free paper.

This book is dedicated to my beautiful wife, Mariana,
and my four children:
Alex, James, Olivia, and Thomas.
And of course,
my mom and dad

TABLE OF CONTENTS

PUBLISHER'S NOTE

This book is intended for practicing attorneys. This book does not offer legal advice and does not take the place of consultation with an attorney or other professional with appropriate expertise and experience.

Attorneys are strongly cautioned to evaluate the information, ideas, and opinions set forth in this book in light of their own research, experience, and judgment; to consult applicable rules, regulations, procedures, cases, and statutes (including those issued after the publication date of this book); and to make independent decisions about whether and how to apply such information, ideas, and opinions to a particular case.

Quotations from cases, pleadings, discovery, and other sources are for illustrative purposes only and may not be suitable for use in litigation in any particular case.

The cases described in this book are composites, and the names and other identifying details of participants, litigants, witnesses, and counsel (other than the author of this book) have been fictionalized except where otherwise expressly stated.

All references to the trademarks of third parties are strictly informational and for purposes of commentary. No sponsorship or endorsement by, or affiliation with, the trademark owners is claimed or implied by the author or publisher of this book.

The author and publisher disclaim any liability or responsibility for loss or damage resulting from the use of this book or the information, ideas, or opinions contained in this book.

INTRODUCTION

The Domino Theory

You have a row of dominos set up, you knock over the first one, and what will happen to the last one is the certainty that it will go over very quickly.

President Dwight D. Eisenhower

Proximate cause is one of the most confusing issues a jury will encounter. I cannot tell you how many times the foreperson has requested the judge reread the definition of proximate cause during deliberations. Knowing this, I reiterate its definition several times during my opening and closing arguments. Proximate cause is a cause that is not remote. It does not have to be the direct cause, but it does have to be a substantial factor in bringing about the resultant accident and injuries. The defendant's negligence (the cause) sets in motion a natural and continuous sequence of events. But for the defendant's initial negligence, these events would not have occurred. There are several definitions of proximate cause. In fact, every State has its own definition. This is also true for the Federal Courts and many legal books and dictionaries. These various definitions all contain the same premise: a proximate cause is a cause that sets a sequence of events in motion.[1]

---

1 The Appendix at the end of this book lists definitions of proximate cause by State, legal treatise, and legal dictionary.

I practice law in New Jersey. I am a plaintiff's lawyer specializing in personal injury cases involving trucking accidents, automobile accidents, and premises liability matters. I have been trying approximately fifteen cases a year for the last ten years—and not only for my firm, but other firms as well. I pride myself on thoroughly understanding the medicine and using analogies to make it simple for the jury.

I do this through a show-and-tell format that simplifies confusing and complex medical and legal concepts—concepts that jurors typically know nothing about and that are about to be thrust upon them. You only have a brief period of time to teach them these very complicated principles. I have practiced simplifying medical and legal principles at trial, in my conference room, in restaurants, bars, in my home, and in my car. I have conducted focus groups, not to determine the outcome or value of a case, but just to learn which medical, legal, or technological demonstration is easiest for juries to understand.

When I first began trying cases, I did not completely understand the proximate cause charge. Notwithstanding, I was still winning a majority of my cases. However, today I probably wouldn't lose the cases I lost then because I have a clearer understanding of proximate cause. New Jersey Courts define proximate cause as follows:

> By proximate cause, I refer to a cause that in a natural and continuous sequence produces the accident/incident/event and resulting injury/loss/harm and without which the resulting accident/incident/event or injury/loss/harm would not have occurred. A person who is negligent is held responsible for any accident/incident/event or injury/loss/harm that results in the ordinary course of events from his/her/its negligence. This means that you must first find that the resulting accident/incident/event or injury/loss/harm to *[name of plaintiff or other party]* would not have occurred but

for the negligent conduct of *[name of defendant or other party]*. Second, you must find that *[name of plaintiff or defendant]* negligent conduct was a substantial factor in bringing about the resulting accident or injury/loss/harm. By substantial, I mean that the cause is not remote, trivial or inconsequential.

If you find that *[name of defendant or other party]'s* negligence was a cause of the accident/incident/event and that such negligence was a substantial factor in bringing about the injury/loss/harm, then you should find that *[name of defendant or other party]* was a proximate cause of *[name of plaintiff]'s* injury/loss/harm.[2]

As you can see, it is no surprise that your average juror, when listening to this charge among the dozens of others, fails to understand it. In fact, many experienced lawyers still don't understand it. After years of attempting to wrap my head around proximate cause, I set out to discover a way to simplify this concept for trial. I came up with the *domino theory*.

During my opening and closing statements, I explain that but for the initial negligence of the defendant, the accident and my client's initial pain and following treatment, diagnosis, surgery, and continuing pain would not have occurred. Thus the defendant's negligence was both a proximate cause of the accident and a proximate cause of my client's injuries. I demonstrate this using dominos that are each labeled with a specific event. You can add as many events, or dominos, to the chain as you need to tighten up your argument. I usually line them up on the jury rail or set up a long table that allows me to fully display what occurred following the defendant's initial act of negligence that ultimately caused my client's injuries. This demonstration is the

2 New Jersey Civil Model Jury Charges available at http://www.judiciary. state.nj.us/civil/civindx.htm

culmination of a consistent theme that I interweave throughout the presentation of my client's case.

This book will take you through a lawsuit, beginning with evaluating your work ethic as a lawyer and onto client intake, prelitigation, the lawsuit's filing, discovery, and trial. I also include how I use the domino theory to demonstrate all of the elements needed to prove a personal injury case: negligence, injuries, permanence, preponderance of the evidence, damages, and proximate cause. I will share not only some of the tactics I created and use at trial, but also some of the effective trial techniques I have learned from my colleagues that I regularly use in the courtroom.

Additionally, this book will explain how to set up your case presuit, as well as during the discovery process, to collect the dominos—or facts and evidence—that you'll ultimately use at trial to prove proximate cause. The domino theory can also assist you in preparing your case for settlement by preparing a pretrial settlement package showing that the negligence of the defendant was a proximate cause of the accident and laying out the resultant accident and injuries in an indisputable chronological format.

1

YOU

When you are inspired by some great purpose, some extraordinary project, all of your thoughts break their bonds, your mind transcends limitations, your consciousness expands in every direction and you find yourself in a new, great, and wonderful world. Dormant forces, faculties, and talents become alive and you discover yourself to be a greater person than you ever dreamed yourself to be.

Anonymous

Being a lawyer is not a job; it's a career. Being a trial lawyer is not a career; it's a lifestyle. You try a lot of cases, you attend and lecture at many seminars, you get involved in the plaintiff's bar associations, you discuss the newest case law with your colleagues and you share information with your brothers and sisters of the plaintiff's bar. You live and breathe the law every minute of every day. You work hard and play harder. Even while at play, you discuss the law over cocktails, tell stories about your cases, and bounce ideas off of anyone that will listen.

Recently, I gave an opening statement in my sleep. My poor wife had to listen to the whole thing. It is not uncommon for me to dream about a trial while I am in the middle of it. I am so consumed with trial work that I live, breathe, and even dream it.

My father, Louis Capozzi, was a linesman for the Long Island Lighting Company. He worked there for forty-six years and he never used a single sick day in his entire career. In fact, when he retired he had forty-six years worth of sick time in the bank. Unfortunately, I never saw much of him growing up because he was always working. He was also a bartender at a bowling alley and had his own catering business with my Uncle Gennaro.

The one possession I did receive when he passed away a few years ago was the ashtray he received as a token for his commitment and dedication to his job for working two million man-hours. It's an ashtray. I still have it and cherish it because it took my father, and his division, the Queens/Nassau County Division, two million hours of hard work to earn it. But that is not all he left me.

I also received his intense and relentless work ethic. My dad was a family man. He was married to my mom for over fifty years, had four kids, and held three jobs just to get us by. He was a big time Mets and Jets fan and always found time to take us to Shea Stadium to see both teams play. He never turned down overtime or a catering job and his work ethic was as rock-solid as his forearms. My mom ran the household. She cooked, is the cleanest person I have ever encountered in my life, and used the threat of "wait 'til your father gets home," which always worked, to keep us in line.

If you do not have a solid work ethic, then being a trial lawyer is not the career for you. I have been a sanitation worker, a landscaper, a tile and marble setter, a contractor, a pizza maker, a pizza delivery boy, a butcher, and a musician. I began working at about age ten delivering papers.

I had two paper routes, the *Daily News* in the morning before school and the *Long Island Press* in the afternoon after school. I would ride my bike with a canvas bag full of newspapers attached to the handlebars of my Schwinn bicycle. I cannot tell you how many times, in the rain and the snow, the weight of the papers made my bike topple over when I was delivering them. Even worse, at night I had to ride my bike to all my customers' houses and beg them to pay the money they owed for the weekly newspapers. I would ring the doorbell and yell, "Collect!"

They would either ignore me or yell back, "I'll pay you next week!" I had this little book that I used to keep track of the money they owed. I mean, the paper was like maybe seventy-five cents for the week, including Sunday, and these people made it so difficult to collect. My pay came out of that money because I had to pay the newspaper companies their money first before I received mine. So I was always behind in my own income because the deadbeats that took the newspapers and waited four, five, or six weeks to pay me, had *my* money.

Little did I know that this was a premonition of the life I would someday lead, chasing insurance companies for other people's money after these companies had taken the premiums for the coverage my clients had selected, been promised, and paid for. When that coverage has been either due to someone else, because the insured injured someone, or has been against my client's own insurance company for uninsured or under-insured motorist coverage, they've used every sleazy tactic in their power not to pay the claim. This has included hiring physicians that have systematically never found anyone injured.

This is why the disdain I hold for the insurance companies is unmatched by any other hatred I have experienced in my life, (except maybe for the Red Sox and Patriots). This injustice is my inspiration. When you are as passionate as I am about forcing insurance companies to pay the coverage they owe, your passion is a force that cannot be stopped.

You must try cases. You must put fear in the minds of the adjusters and defense lawyers. You cannot expedite trials, try cases without experts, cap damages at the policy limits, or enter into high-low agreements. The only risk the insurance companies have at trial is a runaway or an excess verdict. You cannot eliminate that risk.

Insurance companies have lobbied laws that limit your clients' right to sue under the guise that it will save money for the client. In New Jersey we have the AICRA statute, the Automobile Insurance Cost Reduction Act of 1998. AICRA established the limitation on lawsuit option. This option enables insurance purchasers to pay a lower premium for limitations on their right to sue. AICRA also adds an additional hurdle to filing a lawsuit. Pursuant to AICRA section 39:6A-8a, your client must prove that she has suffered an injury that meets one of the six following categories as a prerequisite to having the right to file suit and provide certification from a treating physician affirming one of these six injuries:

1. Death

2. Dismemberment

3. Significant disfigurement or significant scarring

4. A displaced fracture

5. Loss of a fetus

6. A permanent injury

Most drivers select this option as they just want to drive, and don't think about protecting their loved ones or themselves from harm if an accident occurs. Who expects to have an automobile accident? These drivers just want to be legally able to drive a car and get to work and the limitation on lawsuit option is the cheapest way to accomplish just that.

Many lawyers do not accept cases if the limitation on lawsuit option was selected. The reason is that the majority of injury cases are soft-tissue cases such as neck, back, knee, and shoulder tears or spinal disc injuries. As these cases do not fall within categories one through five, they must be proven through category six: permanency. Section 39:6A-8a of AICRA defines permanent injury as the following: "an injury shall be considered permanent when the body part or organ, or both, has not healed to function normally and will not heal to function normally with further medical treatment." You must accept and try these cases.

Any lawyer can win a case where someone suffers an injury within categories one through five. It's the soft-tissue or whiplash-type injuries that insurance companies want to defend. These cases are difficult to win without excellent lawyering skills, knowledge of the medicine, and the money to properly finance a case from beginning to trial and beyond. You need to invest in your cases, emotionally and financially.

Most lawyers refuse to take soft-tissue or whiplash cases because insurance companies force plaintiffs to try them. When attorneys do not accept these types of cases, take a voluntary dismissal at trial, or even worse—settle them for peanuts, the insurance companies win. If your website states that you are a certified civil trial attorney, a member of the Million Dollar Advocates Forum, or you fight for the little guy, then prove it. Go to trial.

When you refuse to take on soft-tissue cases because of an insurance company's policy to try limitation on lawsuit policies, you embolden them. You assure them of what they already know: most personal injury attorneys cannot and will not try cases. They only settle. They are used car salesmen, not trial attorneys. The insurance companies think the majority of us can make a hell of a television commercial but cannot try a case.

I often lecture that the limitation on lawsuit is a myth. It is. Insurance companies do not defend soft-tissue limitation on lawsuit cases on the issue of permanency. They try them on the issue of causation. The insurance company doctors do not opine the injury is not permanent, they opine the plaintiff did not suffer a permanent injury caused by the accident. They opine that the herniated disc was preexisting, not that the herniated disc is not permanent or will heal to function normally. Of course it will not. In fact, proving permanency helps you, the plaintiff's trial lawyer. If you do win on causation, then permanency increases damages. The domino theory will make the defendant's argument weak and ridiculous.

So try cases, and try the good ones. Try the cases with credible clients, decent property damage, and compelling facts. You must try these cases properly and, if given the opportunity by your firm to do just that, you must win more than you lose.

You can't waste opportunity. I recently heard Jim Craig, the goalie for the 1980 United States Olympic Hockey Team, speak at an event. He said that the key to his success, not only during the Olympic Games but also afterwards as a motivational speaker and businessman, was that he was given the opportunity to play and he took advantage of it. This led to all of the great things he achieved in his life. For those young lawyers just out of law school or who have been practicing for a short period of time, I cannot stress it enough: if your firm's partners give you the opportunity to go and try cases, and try them correctly—that means spend money and put on the best case you can—do it. If you have talent, you can write your own book. You can become a heavy hitter in the game of trial advocacy.

The financial and emotional rewards for doing something as great as being a trial attorney are endless. There is no ceiling. But you must do it for the right reasons. You must do it for the injured clients. The rewards you sow, not only spiritually but also economically, will be life changing. I am so thankful that I am a trial lawyer. It is the greatest profession in the world. I wake up every morning, bright eyed and ready to go.

While driving in, I smile all the way to the office listening to music like Led Zeppelin, Nirvana, The Beatles, or Radiohead. I save Black Sabbath, Motley Crue, and Alice in Chains for trials. I am blessed to say I have never worked a day in my life since becoming a trial lawyer. How can something so much fun be work? If you truly enjoy what you do, as stressful and taxing as trial work can be, it will be an adventure, a quest to learn everything you can, and keep you as knowledgeable and prepared as required for excellence.

There was a six or seven year period of my career where I was trying fifteen or more cases a year to conclusion. That does not include some weeks when I'd pick three juries and settle the cases after opening. That occurred on several occasions. I was appearing at trial calls every Monday with three or four cases on the trial list. I was settling the majority of my cases and trying the rest. If I lost I was suicidal. If I won my happiness was immeasurable. It was killing me. I needed to be able to handle losses with the same emotion as I did when I won, so I developed the C. C. Sabathia analogy.

One evening, I was watching the Yankee game and C. C. Sabathia was pitching. He was having a phenomenal year and was the front-runner to win the Cy Young Award. His record was 20–6. I started to think, wow, he lost six times and he is the best. Every five days he takes the mound, and sometimes he is lights out, sometimes he struggles and still wins, sometimes he gets creamed and wins and sometimes he just gets creamed. But every five days he still goes out there and takes the ball.

I was able to view the grind of trials every week or two with this simple sports related thought pattern. This is just like going to court every week: new opponent, new case, new city. Sometimes I massacre my opponent, sometimes I do a good job and win, sometimes I do a good enough job to win and lose, and sometimes I lose badly. But other times I hit home runs.

If you do not get into the batter's box, or are afraid of striking out, you will never hit a home run and feel the greatest feeling you have ever experienced: a verdict. If you are given the opportunity to try cases and want to succeed in this business, then I suggest you take it, or seek out an office that will give you the opportunity. Otherwise, sit on the bench and watch the other players play.

Chapter Takeaways

- ◆ You must make the law your life.

- ◆ You must have a tireless work ethic.

- ◆ You must try cases. The insurance companies know who tries cases and who does not and the offers you receive will reflect it.

- ◆ You must invest financially in your cases to increase your ability to be successful.

- ◆ If the opportunity to correctly try cases is given to you, do not waste it. If it is not given to you, go find it elsewhere.

2

YOUR CLIENT

It is not the employer who pays the wages. Employers only handle the money. It is the customer who pays the wages.

Henry Ford

Your client is expecting a lot from you. It is the only case he has, and he is watching it like it's the only case he has. You have hundreds of cases. He has one. Thus, you have to treat him like he is your only client.

I often tell my clients that I am going to try another case next week, and if they want me to try their case, I am willing to do so. However, I remind them that they could get more than the defense is offering, less than what the defense is offering, the same (minus trial costs), or I could lose and they'd get zero. If the defense is not offering enough and my client's case is solid, I will often talk them into trying it. With most cases, there are usually some problems. No case is perfect. In fact, all of them have at least one or more issues that could destroy the case.

About 95 percent of lawyers have never tried a case. They advertise themselves as trial lawyers—they even advertise that they are super lawyers. They sign up accident victims and have no intention of ever stepping into the courtroom. This is just wrong.

I cannot tell you how many times I have gotten phone calls from attorneys telling me they have a case scheduled for trial next week and it is a "no pay." They ask if I want to try it for them because they couldn't settle it. I tell them that of course, it is a no pay. This is "so and so" insurance company, every soft-tissue case is a no pay. They should have recognized it when they did the intake and reviewed the police report. Then they tell me they were hoping the client would get surgery.

What happens after this is the reason certain insurance companies take this no pay stance. They get to the trial call and the attorney takes a voluntary dismissal. I see it every day in court. The insurance companies know that this lawyer has not taken a case to trial in twenty years and that he is certainly not trying this case. The thing that really upsets me is when, at the last minute, the lawyer tells the client, "I will try the case but you have to pay for the doctors." What client can afford to pay $12,000 for expert testimony? This happens all the time.

It reminds me of my favorite movie scene of all time, the Alec Baldwin scene in *Glengarry Glen Ross*. The coffee is for closers speech. I give this speech often, "You call yourself a trial lawyer? Then prove it." It is no coincidence that the defendant prevails 90 percent of the time on soft-tissue cases at trial. I have seen the logs of cases at the courthouse where they list every trial and the outcome. I have also heard the judges' warnings about the amount of "no causes."

However, the prevailing listed verdicts are often the same lawyers winning over and over. This is because the majority of attorneys who do attempt to try cases, try them half-assed. They only bring in a chiropractor when the defense has an orthopedist and a neurologist. It is no coincidence that the attorneys I know who actually do try cases correctly win at least 75 percent of the time. I see the same attorneys winning soft-tissue trial after soft-tissue trial. Obviously, you have to know what you are doing, but you also have to spend the money.

Many plaintiffs' attorneys whine about justifying the expenses on a trial that they say is worth $25,000. The only parties saying the case is worth $25,000 are the insurance companies and the lawyers who regularly settle them for that much. These same attorneys have been hearing this figure for so long that they actually believe these cases *are* worth $25,000. How you justify paying $12–15,000 for experts and exhibits in a soft-tissue case is by whacking the defendant for $400,000 at trial. In my experience when you win, you win pretty big.

I used to work for a lawyer, Jae Lee, who gave me carte blanche to bring in as many doctors at trial as I wanted. We had a fund called the "doctor fund." This fund began with a $60,000 deposit that originated with a fee from a case we settled presuit. Everyone has one of those catastrophic cases where you make a phone call and the case settles. You do absolutely nothing. I suggest the next time this happens to you, take the money and put some aside for trial costs. That fund will never be depleted. Every case you try, you take the costs from the fund. These costs can be placed back in the fund after you are victorious.

The amount of money you earn from receiving a much higher award via verdict will make up for the money you lose when you are not victorious. I know you cannot win them all, but when you try the case correctly and invest the money in experts and trial exhibits, your chances of winning increase dramatically. The fund we started many years ago still has the same $60,000 in it. I was given the opportunity to try cases correctly, and I am forever grateful to Jae for that.

Clients find lawyers in many ways. Some by word of mouth because their friend or family member had a personal injury lawsuit and the lawyer did a great job. This is the best way for a client to find an attorney. The Internet is becoming the most popular way for a client to find an attorney. My firm receives more and more cases through our website.

However, there is another way clients find lawyers and that is through mail solicitation. I cannot fathom hiring a lawyer because he obtained my police report and mailed me a letter promising me the stars and the moon, including loans and recommending chiropractors. If that is the way a lawyer obtains business then a red flag should go up as soon as the letter arrives. It amazes me that clients actually hire lawyers because of this practice. It is disgusting.

Every time I select a jury, I hear at least one story of how the juror got in a little fender bender accident and received fifty letters from lawyers soliciting their case. These jurors believe most accident cases are fraud and that cases are driven by attorneys and not clients. Mail solicitation is poisoning our jury pools. It must be stopped. Unfortunately, mail solicitation never will stop because clients fall for it every day and the courts, at least in New Jersey, are turning a blind eye to the practice.

Nontrial lawyers often hold themselves out as trial lawyers and do not (nor have they ever) try anything. They take the last best offer, which is sometimes no offer. If you are one of these lawyers, my advice is to refer the case out the minute it comes in your door, before you mess it up. You know what insurance company you are dealing with; it is right in the police report. To hope that the client will have surgery is ridiculous.

I see many cases from "ham and egger" attorneys who ask me to try a case and the file is as thin as a pancake. They have no medical records, no medical legal reports, no economic experts, no life care plans, no photos, no nothing. I think it is clear why they also have little or no business. Though amazingly, clients repeatedly hire individuals like this and some of them do all right financially because they were fortunate enough to get a few cases that could settle for the policy limits even if a monkey was handling them.

You must return phone calls. The number one complaint I receive from disgruntled clients who want to switch lawyers is that their lawyer does not return calls. You have to call your clients, not only call them back, but call them from time to time to keep them abreast of their cases. You can also do this by generating letters, personal letters, not "Dear Client" letters. These letters can go out when various stages of the case are reached:

- "Dear Mrs. Jones, This correspondence is to inform you that we filed a Complaint in your matter and attach a copy of the Complaint."

- "Dear Mrs. Jones, Attached are the Answers to Interrogatories we answered on your behalf based on the information you provided."

- "Dear Mrs. Jones, Your deposition has been scheduled and we would like for you to make an appointment to come in and prepare for same."

These are simple ways to keep in constant contact with your clients and inform them of the progress on their cases. Although much of the work can be done without their input, it is wise to communicate with them and let them know you really care.

My ex-partner Jan had a great way of communicating with his clients, and I also do this from time to time. When he is in the office on Saturdays and Sundays, he calls his clients. Number one, they are happy to hear from him. Number two, they recognize that not only is this man working on their case, he is working on Sunday. I think this is a great way to let your clients know you care about them.

I give every client my cell number. I give out my number because I am often out of the office and I want the client to know they can call me anytime if they want to discuss their case. This also gives me fewer phone calls to return when I get to the office. For the most part, the clients have not abused this process. I do get the occasional 10:30 p.m. on a Sunday night phone call, but overall I think it is a good practice. If you do not want them to have your personal number, get a cell phone just for clients.

You have to make your career about the clients. I have learned not only in the law, but also when I was a musician, that when you do something for the right reasons, the love of the game so to say, good things will happen to you. Success will come financially and otherwise, and you will excel at what you do. The best advertising is when you have a happy client. They tell their friends and family about you and you have a constant stream of business.

When you handle a case for an injured client, you really get to know that person if you take the time to do so. I like my clients. I want them to be compensated. So, I am really excited when I get a fair and reasonable award for them, either through settlement or through a verdict. I understand what they are going through—I have had numerous surgeries from playing sports, including back surgery and a bicep tendon repair, so I know the limitations a serious back injury can cause and the excruciating pain that comes with it. I also understand what effects painkillers and other medications can have on your daily life.

When I first became a lawyer and heard the settlement offers from adjusters, or arbitration awards from practicing attorneys, for a herniated disc, I went berserk. The adjuster would say, "Oh it's a soft-tissue injury; I'll offer you $15,000." Even practicing lawyers at nonbinding arbitrations would say, "I settled one last week for $18,000, so I think that's a fair award." I would then ask the lawyer, "Have you ever had a herniated disc?" Turn towards the adjuster, "Have you?" They would naturally answer in the negative. I would then go on to explain that I have, and if you had offered me $18,000 as fair and reasonable compensation I would have laughed in your face.

You cannot let adjusters dictate what injuries are worth. That's what they think the settlement value is because they have never experienced the pain that is a herniated disc and because lawyers accept those offers every day. I would rather have my leg broken than suffer another herniated disc. It is one of the most excruciating and disabling injuries you can receive. Your lower back is the core of your body and when it is injured you cannot walk, bend, lift, or even think straight—the pain is so unbearable.

Here is a funny story that occurred once at a trial conference in chambers while waiting with the judge, my adversary, and the insurance adjuster for the jury pool to arrive. My client was involved in a pretty serious accident in which she suffered a herniated disc in her neck and received epidural injections and, despite her doctor's good care, was still suffering four years after the accident. The defendant had a $100,000 policy limit and naturally I wanted all of it.

The judge asked if there was any possibility to settle the case. The insurance adjuster blurted out, "It's a limitation on lawsuit, Judge." I responded, "So what?" She then chimed in, "we offered him $19,000, Judge." I then asked, "How about I come over there and snap your neck for $19,000?" She wasn't too thrilled about the offer and the judge, who was smiling, said, "Whoa, whoa, let's not do anything like that."

The case went to trial. I called numerous doctors, effectively cross-examined their defense orthopedist, and they offered the policy limits right before I stood up for summation.

The minute the case settled I called my wife, Mariana, who was nine months pregnant. She told me she was in labor and I rushed to the hospital just in time to see my son James being born. That was a gift from God that day, November 30, 2009, and one of the greatest experiences of my life.

The case is about the client. My wife was nine months pregnant and due any minute and I was still fighting for my client even though I could have settled that case for a little less at any time during the trial. I am not saying that you should put your family and pregnant wife on hold, but you have to be willing to sacrifice some personal matters to make it about the client.

Chapter Takeaways

◆ Your clients are expecting a lot from you.

◆ Your clients trust you with the most important situations in their lives.

◆ You work for the client; the client does not work for you.

◆ You must communicate with your clients and return their phone calls promptly.

◆ You must make your career about the clients. Do this and the rewards will come.

3

CUSTOMIZE THE CASE

If you follow the crowd, you may get lost in it.

Ritu Ghatoury

Every case is different. When you make your career about your clients, your approach to each case must be original and unique. Every Wednesday afternoon my old firm had a lawyer's meeting. At these meetings, we would roundtable cases regarding legal issues, values, medical issues, and discuss upcoming trials. A former attorney in the office would always introduce a case he was about to discuss as a "garden variety" limitation on lawsuit case or a "run of the mill" case. It drove me crazy.

No case is garden variety. There are so many different factors involved, including the vehicles, impacts, injuries, medical treatment, defense carriers, defense lawyers, defendants, and most importantly the clients. When I look at a case, I look for the weakest part and try to reinforce it and make it the strongest part of the case.

If it's a minor impact, I hire a biomechanical expert or I have the bumper taken off the car and get a collision expert or body shop expert to reassess the damage. There is often much more damage underneath the bumper cover than an insurance carrier's auto body shop will repair or include in their estimate.

As you probably know, when someone is in an auto accident, the carrier often attempts to steer the client to their auto repair shop. Here's what happens: the repair shop repairs only what is absolutely necessary on the exterior of the vehicle. They don't make the welds, paint the parts underneath the vehicle, or repair crush zones. The adjuster will then tell you the property damage amount and attempt to minimize the impact of the collision and thus your case's value.

If there is a prior accident, I get a side-by-side film review from a neuroradiologist. When I draw the timeline of the plaintiff's life, I include the prior accident and prior diagnostic testing results. This will make your case stronger because you'll have a before and after MRI or EMG. You will know what the plaintiff's spine looked like three years before the accident.

Because you customized your case around your client's history, the defense expert will have to opine the condition occurred because of degeneration that took place in that short window of time. Defense experts typically testify that the degenerative process takes years to develop. Confront these experts with prior deposition or trial testimony from one of their previous cases. In cases when there has not been a prior accident, you will often find that these same experts will have testified that it takes years, if not decades, for ridging or spurring to occur.

When it comes to damages, you must customize the case. The value of the case is pain and suffering (noneconomic damages) plus economic damages. You want to put as many numbers on the board as possible. There are obvious, often overlooked, economic damages in every case.

Every person that is permanently injured needs a life care plan. If you are permanently injured, you are going to suffer from pain for the rest of your life. There are probable expenses that will need to be addressed and will only be admissible if you obtain an expert, such as over-the-counter and prescription medication, medical devices, physical therapy, procedures such as epidurals, trigger points and branch blocks, even surgery. Hard numbers that will be admissible at trial will increase the case value and give the defense reason for concern because now their exposure is in fixed numbers.

Another less expensive way to customize and improve your damages argument is to multiply the amount of over-the-counter medication your client has to take weekly, monthly, or yearly and add up the costs. If a person is fifty and needs a bottle of Extra Strength Tylenol every month and the bottle costs $7.50, you can multiply their life expectancy (thirty years) times the number of months per years (twelve months times thirty years equals 360 months), multiply that by $7.50 and you just created $2,700 in future medicals. Naturally, some clients take more, some take less, and some take none at all. You have to get creative.

Customizing the case is crucial to the domino theory. We are trying to prove proximate cause, a substantial factor that set in motion the sequence of events that followed the defendant's negligence, including the accident and injuries. In a recent case, I used the fact that my client had not missed a day of work in twenty-five years and had lived 22,000 pain-free days prior to the accident. I included these dominos in the chain of events that occurred prior to the defendant's negligence.

If the client has severe degeneration (usually a much older client) I will have the client's family practitioner, family members, fellow employees, and friends testify as to how active and healthy my client was despite having degenerative disc disease. These are the best witnesses because they are difficult for an adversary to cross-examine. Other than the usual, "you are friends with Mrs. Jones, correct?" or "you work with Mrs. Jones, correct?" There is typically not very much a defense lawyer can do to neutralize a conditional-fact witness.

Your client is the key to the case. What can be more custom than your client? Every person who lives on this earth has a unique story. They are individuals. The life they were leading prior to the accident or incident that is the basis for their lawsuit is the only life they knew. They like certain things and live their lives a certain way. They may not like the things you like, but to them it is their life and it is all they know.

You must utilize the individuality of their life. Sometime it is their job that is unique, sometime it's their family situation, and sometime it's the activities they enjoy in their spare time. You have to make the client real. Call them by their first name and refer to them by their first name when you discuss them. If the client is likeable or credible the jury may award them a verdict based on those traits alone.

One particular client I had loved to hunt, and loved to hunt during every season. In the early winter it was bow hunting, in the late winter it was hunting with a rifle. To us folks from New York or New Jersey, hunting does not have a lot of appeal, nor do I personally have any interest in killing animals, which could be the opinion of many jurors in a metropolis like where I practice.

However, my client was raised in Pennsylvania, and hunting was something he did with his dad as part of his childhood. It was really important to him and it is a very physically demanding hobby. When my client explained how important it was to him, I knew jurors would appreciate his passion. After listening to him explain it so beautifully, I knew a "Can no longer hunt" domino was going on that jury rail.

I have sat across from clients in my office or conference room and thought to myself, "I am trying this case, this lady is incredible. She is so believable." We have all had these clients. They make our job so much easier. But these clients are few and far between.

Most of our clients are not used to displaying their feelings and are not savvy to the prejudices that they will surely experience in a courtroom for merely exercising their constitutional right to a jury trial. They think their case is worth a million dollars, and who knows, maybe it is.

The problem is that they do not know what juries do in court. Juries are unpredictable. They are six (or more) strangers who do not want to be there, are day dreaming half the time, and especially do not like the plaintiff because the plaintiff, or even the plaintiff's lawyer, is the reason they are stuck in a courtroom. You need to not only turn them around to actually like you and your client, you have to spin them 180 degrees around and make them love you so much they give you money. And it can be done.

Fine lawyers win cases every day, despite the negative propaganda regarding trial lawyers and frivolous lawsuits. I believe people are skeptical of the plaintiff when they become jurors. That is why you have to prove to them that your case is big, it is real, and it is not one of those frivolous cases you read about in the news or see on television. Your client has to be credible, your experts must be great, you have to dismantle the defense experts, and you have to be close to perfect as a lawyer. You need a perfect storm to succeed, and customizing your client's case is a way to work towards creating that storm.

The clients are the reason we do this job. Please do not let them down. Get creative and find a way to customize their cases. There is no format or cookie cutter way to work up a case, just an outline of the items you need to prove it. If you do not get to know your client, you may never learn the most important and interesting things about them.

Find the dominos that will support your client's individuality. These custom dominos can be used to prove damages that are a proximate result of the defendant's negligence. Like my client who loved to hunt, every client has some unique hobby or thing they love to do. The more detailed or customized approach you can develop, the more "real" your client becomes in the eyes of the fact finder and the more serious and clear the defendant's negligence becomes. But for the negligence of the defendant, these unique and individual damages would not have occurred. That's why it is important to start collecting your dominos as soon as possible, so the custom theme of your client's case can be clarified.

CHAPTER TAKEAWAYS

- Every case is different.

- Reinforce the weakest parts of your case. If the visible property damage is minimal, dismantle the car and find more damage.

- Utilize your client's unique story to customize your damages.

- Add dominos that detail your client's unique life and hobbies.

4

Collecting the Dominos

I hate quotations. Tell me what you know.

Ralph Waldo Emerson

The first several dominos needed to prove your case are present when your client enters your office for the first time:

- Your client has already experienced degeneration of the disc or soft tissues.

- The defendant has already been negligent.

- The accident has already taken place.

- The air bag has already either deployed or not.

- The ambulance has already come.

- The client has already been to the emergency room and hopefully seen her primary care physician or first treating doctor.

You may even be retained after most, or all, of your client's treatment has been completed. Collecting the dominos may be as easy as collecting medical records from the treatment your client received following the incident.

With regard to treatment, the more serious cases such as death, severe brain injuries, displaced fractures with open reduction internal fixation (ORIF), and so on, take care of themselves. In other words, there is a care path that the client has no choice but to follow. They are typically unable to work and their days consist of physical therapy, testing, doctor appointments, or watching television. Collect the medical records—and that means all of the medical records—including the following:

- Soap notes

- Diagnostic films

- Reports

- Surgery records (including fluoroscopy films)

- Prior primary care records or records from prior accidents

You have to obtain everything, no excuses. If you do this, then these kinds of cases should take care of themselves.

However, with soft-tissue injuries you really have to manage the care of the patient. You have to make sure the necessary objective tests are done and make sure the client informs you when she visits new doctors so you can obtain the records. Most of the time, I tell my client, "You take care of yourself and go to the doctor, and I'll take care of the lawsuit."

There are some clients who need to be reminded. In a soft-tissue case, someone should constantly be in touch with your clients, making sure to obtain the necessary objective medical tests that you will need to prove your clients' cases.

It is very important to stay on top of cases during prelitigation. Most injured clients, the ones who are in pain but not completely disabled, do not have the luxury of not working. They need to be constantly reminded of doctors' appointments and the necessary tests they need. When you get to trial, you are only as good as what you have in your arsenal and what you have provided to the defense in discovery.

I have tried many cases for other firms, and for the most part, the arsenal was well stocked. However, I have also tried cases where I've been informed at trial by way of objection or *in limine* motion that important records, including MRI reports or films proving the injury, were not provided in discovery. Luckily, I have always been able to prevail despite these issues, but only through pure luck and other crazy, extraordinary means.

One particular case had two accidents and two separate lawsuits and the plaintiff's first lawyer had settled the second one. Because defense lawyers do not typically provide pretrial exchanges one week in advance (despite the rule stating you must), I was sandbagged with an *in limine* motion to bar me from recovery for the first accident because the prior lawyer had not apportioned the damages. The defense lawyer claimed that if you suffer a permanent injury to the same body part twice, you cannot claim it again in the second accident. Since the injury from the first accident was a bulge at L5-S1 and the injury from the second accident was a herniated disc at L5-S1, the defense lawyer claimed the plaintiff could not collect damages from a permanent injury for the first accident since she had already collected money from the second accident, because "how could a permanent injury be permanent twice?"

It is not a good feeling to have your case pulled out from under you in the courtroom when you are ready to begin, especially with your client sitting there hearing how careless you, or the prior lawyer in my case, had been during discovery. That's when I pulled a proverbial rabbit out of my rear end. I told the judge that the plaintiff had suffered a permanent injury to her lumbar spine from the first accident and then also suffered a worsening of the same injury, which was also permanent, from the second accident.

I argued that I was only claiming a twenty-one-month permanent injury because the second accident was twenty-one months after the first. I stated that if I had an accident and lost two fingers on my hand, obviously that would be a permanent injury, but then if I was in a second accident and lost my entire hand, then that would also be a permanent injury. I compared this to the plaintiff's spine injury. The second accident made it worse, but her injury was still permanent prior to the second accident. The judge agreed and I was back in the game. I argued the case for twenty-one months worth of damages and won the trial.

In another case, the plaintiff's original attorney had failed to produce the positive MRI results to the defense. In New Jersey on a soft-tissue case under category number six of AICRA, you need objective medical evidence to prove your permanent injury. Typically, we vault the permanent injury with the objective MRI results but according to the statute, objective evidence upon physical exam, a seriously under-utilized way to vault the threshold, may also be used.

Once you prove a permanent injury through objective credible evidence, you can also bring in all injuries that are not permanent. In the above case, the plaintiff had injuries to his back and jaw. Since I lacked objective evidence to prove the back injury, and the TMJ MRI films were normal, I argued that the objective evidence proving the jaw injury was the audible sound of the plaintiff's jaw clicking, which was elicited upon physical exam and still present at the time of trial. I even brought in a stethoscope to prove the clicking. I then proved the back injury as well, not through objective evidence, but only through the plaintiff's subjective complaints. Again, I survived a directed verdict and even received a very generous verdict for my client.

Whenever I am asked to try a case for another firm, my partners often give me a hard time for three reasons. One, even if we prevail the fee is less because of a fee split. Two, we lay out all the money for trial and take all the risk. And three, I have enough cases of my own to try and they are looking out for my health.

I always want to meet the client before I decide whether to accept the offer. If I like the client, I can't say no. Even if the damages appear to be relatively small in the grand scheme of things or according to the going rate for settlement in a soft-tissue case, I will accept the risk and try the case. Sometimes when I appear at trial for another firm or lawyer, the defense will offer me a fair settlement and I can settle the case when they would never have paid the original attorney. The reason for this, I speculate, is the defense carriers are aware of my reputation of trying many cases and they know that I'm not just appearing at trial in order to settle.

I even handled one of the first Hurricane Sandy claims when my brother's beach house, which stood for 150 years, collapsed due to the one-hundred-mile-per-hour winds on the night of the storm. The insurance company denied payment because they said the house collapsed from "dry rot" and not the hurricane. I said, "Seriously? So, if the hurricane hadn't occurred, the house would have fallen down anyway on October 30, 2012?" Eventually, after filing suit and claiming bad faith and every other count I could add to the complaint, they settled during discovery for the entire claim, including lost rental income.

I learned a lot from that case. It does not matter whether it is a human being, a house, a car, a boat, or a building; insurance companies will defend every case on the premise that there was either a complete or partial preexisting issue with the insured object or person.

With regard to soft-tissue cases, the MRI and EMG are the keys to proving your case. You must gather these dominos. The MRI will show the injuries and the EMG will date them.

The EMG findings, if acute or recent, will prove the accident was the cause of the problem. Coupled with the adjacent level of the MRI findings and your client's history and complaints, the

EMG findings should tighten up your causation argument during the domino theory demonstration. The EMG will either be acute: within 1–3 months, subacute: 3–6 months, or chronic: more than six months old. So if your EMG findings are within the first two categories, which it must be to prove it is recent, then you just proved the spinal disc injury is also recent, as the protruded disc material must have irritated the nerve either physically or chemically.

You must make sure the client obtains these tests if indicated by their symptoms and physical examination findings in order to prove your case. If these tests are not indicated, drop the case and move onto the next one. The last thing you want is to have to try a case that lacks objective evidence and thus has no value and appears either frivolous or fraudulent.

The insurance companies love to try these types of cases. My advice is to try strong cases with decent offers, the ones you have the ability to hit a home run on, not the ones that are weak. Try the cases you want, not that they want. When I say decent, I mean the offer is low in the grand scheme of things, and much less than the injury is worth, but much higher than the insulting offers that are equivalent to nuisance value.

The last several dominos concern damages. These include, but are not limited to, lost income, past medical bills, constant pain, future medical bills, and so on. These are the things the client has either lost, has trouble doing, experiences, or owes as a result of the defendant's negligence. All of the treatment and damages that translate into actual dominos should, for the most part, be ready to go before filing suit. Or if you are like me and file suit very quickly, then they should be collected and tweaked during the discovery process.

Before you file the complaint, and there are many philosophies regarding this tactic, you can also create a settlement package and send it off to the defendant's insurance company in an attempt to settle the matter presuit. Some lawyers attach a copy of the unfiled complaint, threatening to file it if the carrier does not make a fair and reasonable offer. You have a better chance of getting struck by lightning twice than settling a soft-tissue case presuit for fair value. The offers are insulting and I find it to be a waste of time, especially with certain insurance carriers. Therefore, my firm does not send a specials package. I file the declaration of war—the complaint.

The next dominos you will need are experts. Call all the treating doctors. Put on the best case you can and utilize every weapon in your arsenal. Go all in. Try it like it is your only case, the last case of your life. It's up to you. You can be the unprepared lawyer who hopes for an offer and relies on better lawyers doing his job for him when he doesn't get it. Or, you can be the lawyer who collects every domino, heads to trial with a full arsenal, and either receives the fair settlement offer the other guy couldn't get or takes the insurance company for the verdict the client deserves.

CHAPTER TAKEAWAYS

- ◆ Start collecting the dominos that have not already been collected as a result of the accident such as the negligence, the air bag, the ambulance, and the ER visit.

- ◆ Set up a system to ensure all of the objective medical tests have been completed and obtained, including the EMG, which can date your injury.

- ◆ Be the lawyer who tries cases and can obtain fair and reasonable compensation via settlement because of your reputation.

- ◆ When you get to trial, you are only as good as what you have in your arsenal.

5

INTERROGATORIES

It is astonishing what power words have over man.

Napoleon Bonaparte

I am obsessed with interrogatories. Interrogatories are a written list of the dominos you are going to use at trial. They contain your client's medical records from before the accident (if they exist), records from after the accident, test results, loss of income, out of pocket expenses, and your lay and expert witnesses. If you want your client to get their head handed to them on the witness stand, then have someone other than yourself answer interrogatories.

When your client answers interrogatory questions, it will most likely be the first time she will have to tell her story under oath. If you want to be a trial lawyer, you should answer your own interrogatories. I cannot tell you how many times I have had to go off on an associate for not answering interrogatories timely and properly.

Any lawyer who has tried a case and seen their client completely dismantled due to sloppy interrogatory answers—answers that were provided by someone who did not understand the meaning of the question, answer, or the consequences of the answer they just typed—will never let anyone else answer their interrogatories again.

My rule is to answer interrogatories within seven days of receipt of the defendant's answer. No excuses. You need to get the case to the finish line. You do not receive compensation for your plaintiff, or legal fees, until the case settles or you go to trial and prevail. It shows the defense you are not messing around. It also places the burden on your adversary to obtain the medical films or any subsequently produced records, limiting their ability to get extensions on discovery and thus gets your case through discovery quicker and on the trial docket faster.

For example, if you provide your interrogatory answers within seven days and supply the defendant with every medical record attached to them, the defense cannot seek a discovery extension 300 days later because they need a film review from their expert. They have had 293 days to do it. Of course you will consent to at least one request to extend discovery, but when they continue to do nothing and seek to further delay the inevitable trial, you will have great ammunition to argue for a denial of their motion to extend discovery.

Interrogatories must be answered by the attorney, contain exhibit tabs, a table of contents, and be velo-bound. These exhibits will be the dominos you have collected and ultimately use at trial. I create a set for myself that I can walk into court with and it is as if I have the entire file with me. You also must amend them constantly if necessary.

In a case I recently resolved, we amended interrogatories over a hundred times. The defense attorney finally told me he was raising the white flag. He said that if he did not receive at least one amendment from me weekly, he was shocked. This attorney was representing one of the most difficult insurance companies to deal with, and they typically do not throw in their policy limits, if ever, until at least the jury is in the box. Relentless advocacy was obviously their reason for changing this stringent company policy.

In my career, I have seen some pathetic interrogatory answers: a one-eighth of an inch high, non-captioned, piece of garbage comes to mind. If the document, and I use that word loosely, was sitting on a desk by its lonesome, you would not even know what file it belonged to. Along with the complaint, which I also obsess over because it is the first document the defense receives from the attorney, the interrogatory answers have to be impressive.

Image is everything. When a defense attorney receives a sloppy set of interrogatories do you think they are intimidated? I'm certainly not. Typos, few exhibits, no cover, and poorly drafted interrogatories are a window into what will ultimately occur throughout the case.

My interrogatories are a thing of beauty. Many a defense attorney has told me at the deposition of my client that they love them because they contain everything the attorney needs for the deposition. They also hate them because they are bound and have to be unbound and scanned into the computer for the adjuster. Once in a while, if I am in a good mood, I will make a non-bound extra copy for them so they can scan that set into the computer and still keep the bound set for themselves.

I have been working on the content of my interrogatories for over ten years. They are based on interrogatory answers I received from Erick Chizmar, an attorney at my first job as a lawyer in Philadelphia. I took Erick's sample answers and began to transform them into what I use today. I continue to tweak and tweak and tweak them until I think I have overcome some of the things I have experienced during trial or to just make them more organized and easier to follow. I say to answer them personally because after drafting the complaint and answering the interrogatories, you are already familiar with the case. This process forces you to learn it. Afterwards, you can easily prepare your client when he is deposed and also have a pretty good feel for how you want to depose the defendants. When you reach the point where you are handling up to a hundred cases at a time, this definitely helps.

When I tried my first several cases (inherited before my own interrogatories had become ripe for trial as the cases were still in the discovery phase) my clients were getting slaughtered on the witness stand during cross-examination. Even when they were telling the truth, the onslaught was so severe that they appeared to be wiggling and writhing and making excuses for the slightest inaccuracy within their interrogatory answers. They looked uncomfortable, as if they were not being forthright. You can only make so many excuses.

The first case I tried where my interrogatories were used, I got a record-breaking verdict on a disc-bulge case with only chiropractic treatment. It is very important to shield your client from cross-examination as it pertains to their interrogatory answers. The easiest way to do this, and I am not going to get too involved here because I am still trying a lot of cases and plan on doing so for at least twenty more years, is to answer the interrogatories in the third person in a general fashion and answer only after an objection. If I am describing the detailed description of an automobile accident, the reason for the objection is that I often use an accident reconstructionist for the explanation of an accident and to opine who was at fault. I also do not want the client's version of the accident to be influenced by anything that may have been discussed with me while performing the intake or in subsequent conversations.

I believe this is effective on cross-examination because the defense attorney must ask the complete question and complete answer while crossing the plaintiff on the witness stand. When the answer is shrouded in legalese, it is apparent that the plaintiff did not actually answer the interrogatories on his own, but did so with his counsel's assistance. The defense does this all the time. Naturally, the ultimate answer has to be accurate and truthful, but a layer of protection shields your client when his answer is enveloped with legal language. Keep the answers general in nature so as not to lock your client into small details. The details can be fleshed out later during deposition.

Most importantly, if you are going to be answering interrogatories with your client, make sure you have all the information, including how the incident actually occurred. If they tripped, say they tripped; if they slipped, say they slipped. The small details involving how a slip and fall accident occurred can win or lose your case. These answers ultimately become the dominos that will be laid out in chronological order for the jury during the domino theory demonstration.

Answering your own interrogatories is not a difficult task to complete. As I stated earlier, and it is worth repeating, answering your own interrogatories instead of pawning them off on someone else forces you to learn the file. Another thing that you will accomplish by drafting your own interrogatory answers is that you can see what you do not have, what expert reports you need, who you will need to depose, who you may have to subpoena at trial, and how you need to prepare your client for their deposition. You'll begin to understand and learn the case. I begin to lay out the dominos in my head during this time period.

When you answer interrogatories, remember that every case is unique. You have to customize your case and find the facts that support the domino theory. If your case has lost income, you need to show that loss of income through tax returns, pay stubs (pre- and post-accident), and even employee records such as reviews and recognition your client may have received before the accident but not afterward. These are great dominos to use before the defendant's negligence caused the accident, your client's injuries, and her lost income.

Typically, the dominos can remain the same. It is the facts that support each domino that need to be adjusted for every case. If you are going to present the dominos in your closing, you can describe the details that support a general domino such as "lost income." This information should be described during deposition, supported by documentation you provided in discovery, and utilized at trial. Depositions are extremely important for creating custom dominos to prove your case.

Chapter Takeaways

- Answer interrogatories within a week of the defendant's answer.

- Answer the interrogatories yourself to help familiarize yourself with the file.

- Image is everything. Send a well written and proofread copy of your interrogatories, either velo-bound or in a binder complete with table of contents, which allows for easy identification for yourself and the defense counsel.

- Amend interrogatories as often as possible to show the defense counsel you are on top of your case.

6

DEPOSITIONS

Whatever you do, do it to the purpose; do it thoroughly, not superficially. Go to the bottom of things. Anything half done or half known, is in my mind, neither done nor known at all. Nay, worse, for it often misleads.

Lord Chesterfield

Just like the interrogatories that I always tweak, I always seek new ways to better prepare my clients. I show them videos of how a deposition works, send letters to remind them of the deposition, and ask them to make an extensive list of all of the problems they are experiencing, including specific examples of events that caused them trouble, discomfort, or pain. I do not want to hear, "I can't carry the groceries or carry the laundry anymore." I have heard that identical complaint ten thousand times and so have the defense attorneys.

I want specific examples of events. For example, "Yesterday, I was driving the car to the supermarket and I had to pull over and call my husband because the pain in my back was so unbearable

I could no longer drive. I had my kids in the car. A police officer stopped and asked me if I was okay and should he call an ambulance, but I just wanted to wait for my husband. The police officer was so kind, he waited there with me until my husband arrived. My husband eventually came and we left my car in the parking lot of the gas station and he drove me and the kids home." Now that's what I am talking about. A story.

At my old firm, we had a constant debate at our weekly meetings whether our clients needed more preparation for depositions. In most cases, my thought was no, an hour to an hour and a half should be fine. In more complex cases however, you might need to prepare several times over a couple weeks before the depositions. The bottom line is: it is the first time the defense lawyer, on behalf of the insurance company, gets to put a face to the complaint and answers to interrogatories. Your clients should dress appropriately, as if they are going to a job interview. A good presentation is key to getting a favorable settlement offer, although with some insurance companies it doesn't matter if you have Mother Teresa for a client, they are not going to offer anything.

THE DEPOSITION OF THE PLAINTIFF

The deposition of the plaintiff should be simple. Tell the truth, the whole truth and nothing but the truth. So help you God. However, it usually has been a few years since your client's accident, injuries, and extensive treatment with various doctors. Most clients do not remember the dates of treatment—this is normal. They also do not remember the names of the doctors who treated them, their complaints when they presented to them, or their doctor's specialties. You must review the medical records and discuss them with your client, especially the emergency room records, to see what the actual initial complaints were at that time. Often, the injuries that turned out to be the most serious are not even mentioned in the emergency room records.

You must discuss the accident with the client. Although the accident might have been very straight forward, a talented defense attorney will break down the moments before the collision or fall to split seconds and often get an unprepared client to admit they never saw the other car prior to the collision, insinuating they were not making proper observations just prior to the accident. Also review the police report to see what the speed limit is in the area of the accident.

Research the Scene of the Accident

Most importantly, go to the accident scene. I cannot tell you how many times, just by going to the scene of the accident, I have discovered inclines or declines, curves in the road, parked cars obstructing views, road markings, or bushes and hedges that make it impossible to see a car coming across an intersection. This is a must. It allows you to intelligently discuss the accident and scene with your client and ultimately the jury who may live in the area and know it well.

Sometimes you learn other facts that could help you during trial. You can even run into witnesses who may have seen what happened. I often drive past the accident site on my way to the courthouse during a trial, just to continue familiarizing myself with the scene. In a premises case, go several times if you can get access to the location, then set up a formal inspection with your expert.

In one particular case early in my career, when I was handling criminal matters as well as civil, I represented four young Russian guys, all hockey players, who beat the crap out of this little accountant in a strip club. It was two nights before the trial and I wanted to see the strip club so I could understand what the layout of the club was and how I could better defend these guys.

So I strolled into the strip club and there was a very large square bar that left very little room between the bar and the club's four walls. Two people walking in opposite directions along the perimeter of the bar couldn't pass each other in the three to four feet available. And with the bar stools there, the space was very confined. The strippers were on a smaller stage in the middle of the large square. One defendant told me the accountant had attacked him and he had had nowhere to retreat to because of the confined space and thus had to defend himself. The other three had then gone to the aid of their friend.

So I sat down, ordered a drink, and surveyed the layout of the bar. It was just as the clients had described: very tight quarters. Then to my surprise, I saw the accountant sitting two stools away from me, drinking and having a merry old time. He was carrying on, stuffing money into the g-strings of the strippers, doing shots, and being very loud and boisterous.

Two days later when he appeared in court, he was dressed like an accountant with the suit and tie, glasses—the whole routine. He looked like a little angel. He testified on direct examination that he was unable to go out socially anymore because he was afraid he would be assaulted again, and that the beating had affected him psychologically. He was not only looking to have my clients put in jail, but to obtain restitution for his medical bills for the plastic surgery he needed to repair his face. He went on to describe how it was dark and that he was thrown onto the ground by one of my clients while the others kicked him and punched him. He actually demonstrated the beating by lying on the ground and covering his head with his arms imitating how he had had to protect himself from this brutal onslaught.

When it became time to cross him I could barely contain myself. I first got him to admit he could not identify any of the other three men who kicked or punched him as his positioning made it impossible to actually see who was doing the kicking and punching. I then went on to his fear of going out at night and asked him if he recognized me. He said he did not.

I said, "I was sitting two stools away from you last Wednesday night at the strip club. Isn't it true you were out just two nights ago at the very place you claim you were assaulted?" He bowed his head and said yes. All his credibility instantly drained from his body. I then went on to badger him regarding his attacking my client and throwing the first punch and how crowded it was and how there was no room for the defendant to retreat.

The case was dismissed against three of the defendants and the fourth defendant was found not guilty. That was all possible because I went to the scene. Obviously, all scenes are not as fun as the one I just described, but they are priceless for the amount of information you can obtain by just going and looking at them.

In addition to going to the scene of the accident, I always perform a Google Earth search of the accident scene and print it out in various sizes in order to clarify testimony regarding distances and points of interest in the area, including the point of impact. At the deposition, I use these images to examine the defendant. This should always be videotaped; you will never lock them into an explanation of the accident if the deposition is not videoed.

At trial, I blow the images all up and mount them on magnetic boards with a dozen or so small magnets that are shaped like cars. I have the cars made the same size as the cars in the aerial photograph, so they are exactly to scale. I have had attorneys object to the aerial shot and cars, arguing they are not to scale. You should see their faces when I tell the judge they are exactly to scale and then show him a magnetic car fitting exactly over the image of the car on the board. Overruled!

Premises Liability Cases

I think it is important to discuss my feelings regarding a premises liability case, in particular a slip and fall case. The client better know what caused them to fall. If it was a liquid, they need to know and be able to answer the following:

- Were your clothes wet?
- Which foot slipped?
- How did you fall?
- Why didn't you see the liquid on the floor?
- What type of liquid—water, soda, oil, what?
- Were there any characteristics of the liquid that could show it had been there for an extended period of time?
- Were there track marks through it?
- Was it discolored?
- Was it warm to the touch?
- If it was ice, was it partially melted?
- These things are absolutely necessary to prove negligence in a slip and fall case.

THE DEPOSITION OF THE DEFENDANT

Obviously, the type of case determines what you need to obtain from a defendant. In auto cases, I take the shortest depositions of the defendant possible. I get them to admit fault and when they do, I stop. I do not need to know their educational background, whether they are married and have kids, or where they live. I just want them to admit what they were doing was either unreasonable or negligent. I flat out ask them, so the accident was your fault? Then the objection comes and I tell them they can answer. Then they say, "yeah." Deposition over.

When they do not come along so easily, I break out the driver's license test booklet and quiz them on the rules of the road. I ask them if they had to read this booklet before they took their road test. I ask them some of the basic questions regarding following too closely, yielding to traffic when at a controlled intersection, and obeying the speed limit.

I use the classic example of, "You realize that when you are driving behind someone you have to keep a safe distance and travel at a safe speed? That the reason for this is that if a ball rolls out into the street and a small child runs after it, the vehicle in front of you may have to stop suddenly. Thus, you have to stop suddenly. Now in this case, you claim the vehicle in front of you stopped suddenly, correct? Were you traveling at a safe distance? Were you traveling at a safe speed? Were you paying attention? Then how come you couldn't stop?" There is no answer that could justify why they rear-ended your client. Also, do not forget about weather conditions that may require the defendant to act even more reasonably.

I even had a defendant claim, when asked if she ever had any prior accidents, that she had but it wasn't her fault because she'd been rear-ended. I then asked, "So in this case, since you rear-ended my client, the accident must be your fault?" She tried to weasel out of it, but ultimately admitted it was her fault.

DEPOSING EXPERTS

Effectively deposing an expert can help settle your case quickly. I always depose experts. In the auto accident forum, defense medical experts tend to be retained by defendants in several hundred cases a year. I may have a particular expert in several of my cases. The custom, in the auto universe, is not to depose the experts. This is why I do depose them. I depose them on video so when they seem uncomfortable I can show their answers to the jury, displaying their discomfort, which obviously does not show up on a transcript. I have had experts literally pause for 5–7 seconds or more before they answer every question. In the transcript, you cannot truly appreciate this, but on video it is quite clear the expert is trying to think of how to answer the question without being snared in a trap.

If I have a defense expert on several of my cases simultaneously, which is often, I usually only need to depose him on one of the cases. I choose the weakest case with the weakest attorney defending. This practice saves costs, as medical expert depositions can be pricey.

I do this to set the expert up for trial. I want him to contradict his reasoning in the case I am deposing him on because it is the polar opposite of his reasoning in other cases the defense has retained him for. It is amazing how often these guys contradict themselves from case to case. They often claim a plaintiff cannot be injured if they did not go the emergency room as the pain would have been excruciating and thus they could not have been injured. The next case where the client is taken by ambulance to the emergency room complaining of pain that is a 10 out of 10 on the VAS scale, they are also not injured according to the same defense doctor.

The Discount Double-Check

My notice for the deposition of a defense expert requests several documents. They often appear without those requested documents. I also bring boxes of documents. You should see their faces when I roll in with a hand truck full of boxes. I want to produce documents which the expert will identify so at trial he cannot claim he never saw them. I want him to think I am going to depose him on the facts of the case that he is being deposed on, as I mentioned earlier, and then do not ask him a single question about that case. I want to bring an associate or another lawyer from another firm with me, and depose him for hours. I call this the *discount double-check.*

What we do is this, I depose the doctor for two to three hours while my associate is listening and keeping notes, filling in the blanks I may have missed. I then take a break and let my associate take a whack at him for an hour or so. I then come back and finish him off. By the time I complete the deposition, the doctor is so worn down that he gives most of the answers I sought at the beginning of the deposition just to get rid of us. It also allows a second individual to explore areas in cases they may have that are different from my case or theories that differ from mine. It is a great system and everyone should be doing this. I have had lawyers object and jump up and down, but we don't get much push back most of the time.

The discount double-check can also be used on a particular type of specialty expert deposition. This is the expert who is not on hundreds of cases a year, has usually been retained in a medical malpractice or a premises case, and is often a medical specialist or an engineer.

Usually, firms have lawyers with different areas of expertise; some law firms may even have lawyers that are also physicians like mine does. The discount double-check deposition system allows the physician/lawyer to depose the defendant physician in a medical malpractice case, or a medical malpractice defense expert on certain areas of medicine, and allows me or another lawyer to depose the expert on medical legal issues or other areas of medicine. It is the two heads are better than one philosophy.

The discovery deposition, like I mentioned earlier, allows you to explore areas with the doctor that a jury will not hear. I like to play dumb, like Columbo, pretending I do not understand the medicine and have him explain it to me. I like to ask questions like, "doctor, can you please explain this to me?" or "doctor can you explain that to me?" They often pat themselves on the back and puff out their chests as they proudly educate me on the very issue that will later lead to their virtual destruction.

I must state that for the most part, I have the utmost respect for physicians and do not take deposing them or suing them lightly. In fact, I reject 99.9 percent of the medical malpractice inquiries that come through my door. It is the defense expert I do not respect, not straight shooters or real doctors. When my client is sent a defense medical exam notice, I immediately know what the defense doctor's report will say before the exam is even performed. I despise the doctors who have drafted 10,000 reports and never found a single person injured. These are the ones I seek to destroy, to eliminate, to make sure they do not do this again, not only to me, but to every lawyer who has to put up with this nonsense.

Understand the Literature

Again, the key to winning soft-tissue cases is not to make the battle their experts versus your experts. The key is to make it their experts versus the entire medical community. This can be achieved by learning and using the medical literature that is relied upon by every doctor in their field, including the literature published by the defense expert's own specialty boards like the AAOS. It amazes me how often defense doctors spout out information and cite articles that are against them and claim they support their positions. This information has to be clarified for the jury and you, as the trial lawyer, have to be the one to shove it right back down the doctors' throats. You are not always going to get a knock-out punch, but when they are elusive and nonresponsive, that is usually good enough to get your point across to a jury.

Whenever a defense report contains a medical article citation, you must either demand a copy of it or obtain it yourself. Read it several times and understand it. There are often many reasons the article cited, or just the passage cited, is incorrect or irrelevant to the facts of your case. Ask them about the article or position they are taking without showing them the article. Then take out the article and show the good doctor how incorrect he is and how the article does not quite say what he proposes. This can only be accomplished when you have researched the medicine and have come to understand it completely.

There are attorneys from other firms that I get together with regularly. One in particular is Arthur Lynch, whom I adore as a person and an attorney. We break down medical literature, trials, defense experts, jury selection, and books written by other attorneys. We have them all. Any topic we think we can learn better, we explore. In fact, when I'm driving to court or the office in the morning, I often call him and we speak for sometimes hours about issues in cases. He is the only one I know crazy enough to be awake when I am driving to work and often he is already at his desk in his office. Arthur is my morning guy and Michael Maggiano is my evening guy.

In the evenings, around ten or eleven, when I am pacing around the house smoking and thinking about my cases, I often call Michael Maggiano. Like clockwork, he answers the phone and is either still in his office or on the treadmill at the gym near his office. We discuss all the latest and greatest case law, crossing medical experts, and often plan "plaintiffs only" seminars for our brothers and sisters of the plaintiff's bar. Michael has become like a father to me. I love him and his wife, Alice.

Another attorney who prides himself on collecting medical literature, and who I often reach out to when I am in need of a certain type of article is Walter Faust. If a defense medical expert is unlucky enough to have Walter after them, then their time as an expert is usually not long for this earth. Walter has a habit of targeting a defense expert and annihilating him. He has a few defense dentists in his cross hairs, and he is the go to guy regarding dental cases.

I recently sat in with Walter on a deposition of a notorious defense orthopedist. The defense attorney and the doctor, who I know well, were wondering why I was there. It was not my case and I had nothing to do with the case. The doctor must have asked me five times if I didn't have something better to be doing. I said, "what could be better than sitting in and listening to you explain medicine?" My job was to hand the doctor the medical articles Walter and I had organized and marked for the deposition. I left the deposition in awe of Walter's knowledge of the literature and medicine. Lawyers like Walter, Michael, and Arthur inspire me to work harder and become better at what I do.

Lawyers who learn to perfect their craft are present in every state. They are a rare breed but they are out there. That is why it is necessary to join your state plaintiff's bar and get to know individuals like this. We are stronger when we are united. We are in competition with each other, but also teammates. It is an unusual dynamic being personal injury lawyers and working together. It is like Mantle and Maris chasing Babe Ruth's home run record in 1961. Both were competing for arguably the most coveted record in baseball (some would argue DiMaggio's fifty-six game hit-streak was more coveted) but they did it side by side with the ultimate goal of winning. When one of us wins, we all win. It is the greatest profession in the world.

Learning the medicine and collecting and reading the literature will enable you to prepare for the expert deposition. The deposition should not only focus on the literature that pertains to the medical issues in the case but should also focus on the defense medical exam. The defense medical exam is where the rubber meets the road.

CHAPTER TAKEAWAYS

◆ Depositions do not need to be long and drawn out. Know what you need and get right to the point.

◆ Prepare your client to testify to actual examples of problems they are having instead of generalizing.

◆ When deposing a defendant, be prepared to take out the the driver's test booklet and other rules of the road.

◆ Use documents during expert depositions in order to familiarize the doctor with the literature so he cannot deny he has never seen it at trial.

◆ When possible, utilize two attorneys to take the deposition as two heads are better than one.

◆ Bounce ideas off attorneys who you respect and try to work together whenever possible.

◆ Join your state and national trial lawyers associations to see how the best do it.

7

DEFENSE MEDICAL EXAMS

A friend is one who has the same enemies you have.

President Abraham Lincoln

There is no bigger joke than the defense medical exam. I do not even have to read the reports when my clients attend them. Whether the plaintiffs are sixteen or ninety, these exams almost always conclude that they're suffering from a preexisting condition of some sort. I also love the way these doctors will cherry pick any inconsistency out of records that will often cover several years and thousands of pages. They also tend to conveniently leave out all of the most serious complaints and findings.

As I explained earlier: when there is no emergency room visit, the defense doctors will claim that because the plaintiff didn't experience any immediate pain and didn't visit the emergency room, she must not have been injured. However, if you collect all of these experts' reports, you'll discover that even when there is emergency room treatment, they will opine that it is of no significance. When the plaintiff experienced pain that was ten out of ten on the VAS scale, they leave it out. When disc herniation compressed the spinal cord, they leave it out. When there were positive objective findings from physical exams with several treating doctors, they leave it out.

I inform my clients that this is what they should expect from a defense medical exam. I tell them not to exaggerate and remember this guy is not your friend. He will typically be very nice to you, try to make you relaxed, agree that you are injured, and then write his report that you are a liar, a malingerer, and a fraud. He will request you fill out a long questionnaire that is more like answering interrogatories than filling out an intake form, ask who referred you to your doctors, and all about your prior accidents and injuries. He will be watching you when you arrive, get up to greet him, walk down the hall, and when you get up on the examining table. He will examine you for five minutes, then watch you leave. Some of these sleaze balls actually look out the window and watch clients walk to and get into their cars.

You must prepare your client as best you can. Most clients get the picture but many fall for the fake personality and friendly manner. There are many attorneys, including myself, who request all intake forms prior to having the client attend the defense exam. This way the information can be filled out with the assistance of counsel. Why a defense doctor needs answers to interrogatories, the police report, photos of the car, and property damage estimates, is beyond me.

That alone should be a red flag to jurors that this man is not acting in the capacity of a doctor. He is acting like a defense detective. I have been to a few doctors in my day and have never been asked for those things. Instead, the doctors ask me what happened. I tell them and they treat me. That is the way medicine is and should be. The patient's complaints should tell most of the story.

Many lawyers, but not me, send a nurse to attend and witness the defense exam. I personally think this is counterproductive as the doctor should be on his best behavior with a medical professional witness present, but you would be surprised how arrogant some of these doctors still are. Despite a nurse noting every word the client says, and recording each and every test the doctor performs, some doctors will still draft a report misquoting the client and claiming they performed tests they did not. This does not happen often. Most doctors are smarter than that, but it does actually happen from time to time.

In one particular case, a client tape-recorded the entire exam. It lasted ninety seconds. When the doctor testified that he had examined them for fifteen or twenty minutes he was crucified on the stand with the ninety-second audiotape. (Whether or not a secret tape recording is permissible depends on the state in which the exam took place and the relevant law.)

The defense will argue that their medical exam is a series of allegedly objective tests. They are all subjective. When your client complains of pain on a particular test, the defense doctor will claim it is a subjective finding and thus meaningless. When your client does not complain of pain, the test is normal. The client cannot win.

I can barely contain myself at trial when the defense doctor testifies about his physical examination of my client. The doctor must use the word "normal" at least twenty-five times. When a complaint of tenderness or pain is elicited, the doctor quickly dismisses it as, "oh that is a subjective complaint." The reality of the matter is the test is either "normal" or your client complains and it's "subjective."

This little trick drives me crazy and must be exposed at trial. I often ask doctors at deposition or trial whether each test, in and of itself, either rules in or rules out a herniation or bulge. I go down a list of each test and have the doctor explain how he does each one. Some of these tests are downright ridiculous.

For example, neurologists begin their exams by checking a patient's eyes, tongue, balance, and so on. I ask them how they perform this test. They'll testify, "I ask the patient to stick out their tongue."

I then retort, "like this?" And I stick out my tongue.

The doctor will state," yes, just like that."

I then ask, "Does that test rule in or rule out a herniated disc in my client's back?" The answer is obviously no. I then run through the battery of tests they perform and have them confirm that each test, in and of itself, neither rules in nor rules out a herniated or bulging disc. I developed this line of questioning with Arthur Lynch. He came up with the isolation of each test and I came up with mimicking the exam. Teamwork is essential in this business.

Below is a cross-examination of a defense orthopedist regarding his report from his exam of my client. Well, not actually my client, my friend's client. I tried this case for a really good friend of mine and I always laugh when I think about how I came to try it.

I was at the trial call for one of my own cases and it settled. Afterward, my friend pulled me aside and said he was assigned out for trial. He asked if would I go into the judge's chambers and tell the defense counsel that I was trying the case because I had just received a verdict against this insurance company the week before. He continued that the defendant only had a $25,000 policy and that if I walked in, they would pay it.

I said I wasn't so sure about that but waltzed into the judge's chambers ready to settle the case. The defense counsel stated that it was a "no pay." I suggested she pay the policy because I was trying the case. She reiterated that they were offering zero. The client, who didn't speak English, was pretty injured with a shoulder issue and a herniated disc in his back with epidurals—one that punctured his thecal sac. I did not know the facts of the case at the time, but I told my friend, "give me that file, I am trying this case. Call the doctors, all of them."

He said, " But Ed, I have been saving my money so I can take my family to Disney World next week. I can't pay for all of the doctors."

I told him to, "just get the money and pay them. I am going to win this case and you will get your money back and have an even better time at Disney World."

Meanwhile, I had not even looked at the file nor met the client. I was just so furious with this insurance company and especially this defense attorney and her smug attitude that I wanted blood. However, in the back of my mind I was so nervous I could lose the trial, fail the client, and my good friend would not be able to take his kids to Disney World. He reluctantly paid for four doctors. The defense had scheduled one: an orthopedist whom I had heard of but had never crossed.

As we selected the jury I was reading the transcripts and reviewing the file. By the time the jury was in the box I was ready to go. When I did my opening statement I knew the case cold as if it were one of my own. This excerpt from the cross-examination of the defense's orthopedist is about the defense physical exam he gave our client. It begins with me reading from his report:

Q: Let's talk about his neck. There were no spasms or tenderness… so you didn't feel any "lumps" or "bumps" [these were the words he used to describe spasm on direct exam] in his neck. There was normal alignment, full range of motion, and so on. So in other words when you were working on his neck were you actually twisting it or were you asking him to do it?

A: I was asking him to do it.

Q: Okay, so he didn't exaggerate or do anything that you thought was not credible?

A: No.

Q: Okay. Next you examined the right shoulder and found full range of motion, correct?

A: Correct.

Q: Now you examined the left shoulder and wrote, "examination of the left shoulder revealed some suboptimal effort." So in other words you were telling him to raise his shoulder and he did not raise it high enough for you, is that what you're saying?

A: Well, he didn't go as far up as the right shoulder.

Q: Well that's the shoulder where his injury is, isn't it?

A: I didn't find any injury to the shoulder.

Q: You didn't, but he's claiming an injury to the shoulder. He testified he injured it and every other doctor has agreed that it happened. You disagree?

A: Well he's claiming an injury, so when I asked him to raise his shoulder on the active range of motion he went only to a certain degrees—minus 20 degrees which is less than full. The right shoulder is 170 and the other one is a little less. Not a big difference. But if he's complaining of discomfort I am not going to force the shoulder, but I was kind of surprised. There was no reason why he could not move the shoulder.

Q: Are you living inside this person's body?

Defense counsel: Objection, Your Honor.

Judge: He can answer.

Q: Are you?

A: Am I? No.

Q: So if you say, "Lift your arm," and he lifts it as high as he can because it hurts, you're going to say he didn't lift it high enough?

A: I recorded what he could lift and what his complaint was.

Q: Yeah, and you said he used "suboptimal" effort?

A: Because I found no physical block as to why he couldn't lift it all the way up.

Q: Except his pain?

A: That's subjective.

Q: Did you see the MRI?

A: Yes.

Q: There was tendinopathy, there was effusion, and he's telling you his arm hurts, correct?

A: I found no effusion; there was normal fluid in the joint. I found mild tendinopathy. I essentially agree with the radiologist. There is a little bit of signal change, but it's not consistent with the injury.

Q: So the right arm is normal and the left is abnormal?

A: Well, minimally, because he's lacking a few degrees.

Q: Okay, now let's go down where it says "neurological exam of the lower extremities reveals strengths to be normal and sensations to be intact to pin prick at light touch." What do you do, run a feather along his foot or something?

A: A pin-prick is a dull pin we use and we use a pinwheel and the light touch is touching the skin lightly.

Q: What part of the skin are you touching?

A: Over the various dermatomes in the leg.

Q: Did he take his pants off?

A: I rolled his pants up.

Q: Did he have to take his shoes off?

A: He had his shoes off.

Q: Had his shirt off too?

A: Yeah, sure.

Q: Okay, now you said, "examination of lower back reveals normal lumbar curve, there was no spasm or tenderness, full range of motion and all arch was present." How do you do that? Do you perform a sitting straight-leg test?

A: That's not the back part that's the neurological part.

Q: Okay, so what do you do on the back to show full range of motion?

A: Ask him to bend forward, "as far as you can go," and then they have the rotation.

Q: Did he say, "ooh ahh ohh"?

A: No.

Q: Was he exaggerating?

A: If you exaggerate you have a complaint, he didn't have a complaint.

Q: Exactly, but if he did, that would've been subjective right? If he would've said, "Ouch that hurts," that would've been subjective right?

A: It is a subjective remark.

Q: There is no objectivity to the test right? There's no objectivity to any of these tests, correct?

A: There are, you can detect spasm, you can detect atrophy, you can detect restriction of motion.

Q: Well ironically, you mention lack of spasm. Six months later, Dr. Dubrow did an exam and said "severe bilateral spasm in his lower back," and when you examined him he had none. Is that true?

A: Correct.

Q: So maybe it's you that is being subjective?

A: That's incorrect.

Q: And, if he cried out during one your so-called objective tests, it would've been subjective and if he doesn't cry out its normal, right?

A: Well normal is normal, it's normal not to have pain but when somebody says they have pain it's a subjective complaint. You have to correlate that with objective findings on the examination.

Q: No doctor, you have to... isn't it true that you do not just rely on the physical examination only, you have to rely on the history, the complaints, the diagnostic tests, which there were two in this case?

A: Yes.

Q: And isn't it true that MRIs are objective?

A: Yes.

Q: An EMG is also objective: it's a diagnostic test. Objective test right?

A: Not totally, because depending on the training and experience of the performer. In other words, with an MRI I can read it. An EMG we are always depending on the reader, the performer.

Q: You can't read it?

A: Right.

Q: In other words it's not objective to you, its objective to the person who is trained to read them, and you can't read it?

A: Depends on the training and skill.

Q: A Board certified neurologist—you have any reason to believe he doesn't know how to read it?

A: That's not what I said.

Q: What did you say? Depends on his skill?

A: That's what I said.

Q: So is it objective or not?

A: It's subjective in what his reading is. It's not objective in that I can read it and confirm it.

Q: Because you are not trained to do it, that's why it's not objective to you, correct?

Defense counsel: Objection Your Honor, can we keep the comments to ourselves?

Judge: (giggling)

Mr. Capozzi: That was a question.

Judge: Really? What would be the answer be to that?

Mr. Capozzi: The answer would be "yes," since he admitted he has no training in interpreting EMGs.

A: That's not the answer, no.

Q: So, you *are* qualified to read an EMG? You just said you were not.

A: I said I was not. I'm dependent on somebody else to read it for me. As I said before, I cannot take it into consideration by itself.

Is this guy for real? He thought objectivity is based on whether *he* could interpret something? I went on to win that trial for my friend, and quite convincingly, with a verdict over six times their policy limits and my buddy got to take his family to Disney World. I really wanted to win that case—not just for him and his family, and the client and his family—but for the principle. This doctor is one of the worst, deceptive defense doctors in New Jersey.

You can cross a doctor on the medicine and the defense medical examination. Most lawyers will tell you to never cross a doctor on medicine, that he will cream you. I disagree. When you use common sense and couple it with the plaintiff's history and the findings of the treating doctors, it is clear how useless these defense exams are. The examinations are a ten-minute investigation of the plaintiff's claim, not an independent medical examination as claimed by the defense. What doctor ever needed to see photos of a car to diagnose what injury one of his patient's suffered? They ask you what happened and you tell them.

CHAPTER TAKEAWAYS

- The defense medical expert is usually the only hurdle you must get over in order to prevail at trial for your client.

- You should collect all of a defense examiner's defense medical exam reports you can locate because defense doctors typically contradict themselves from case to case.

- Prepare your clients for the defense examination. Make sure they are prepared to answer written questions and that their answers are consistent with their deposition testimony and interrogatory answers.

- Advise your clients to be truthful regarding prior accidents and injuries and not to exaggerate their pain levels.

- Challenge the doctor on the medicine at trial if you understand it.

- Use common sense, your client's history, and the findings of your client's treating doctors to disprove the defense doctor's opinion.

8

SETTLEMENT AND MEDIATION PACKAGES

It's the perfect definition of a settlement. Both parties did not get what they wanted.

David Geffen

The settlement package is thing of the past. And I do not mean a mediation or arbitration settlement package. I mean a prelitigation settlement or specials package that is sent to the insurance adjuster to settle a case presuit. I have never drafted one, do not believe in speaking with adjusters, and only want to file a complaint and get the ball rolling.

Older attorneys speak of the glory days of making a phone call and settling a soft-tissue case for one hundred grand. They also speak of the days where an insurance adjuster would come to the office and settle ten or fifteen cases over lunch. They would be wheeling and dealing.

Those days are over. So are the days of sending a specials package to an adjuster and not only hearing back from them, but hearing back from them with a fair and reasonable offer. Today, you get a song and a dance from an adjuster and they low-ball you with a ridiculous offer. They go on to tell you how when their insured turned left into your client, your client could have swerved and braked and honked his horn, so the liability split should be sixty-forty.

I detest speaking with adjusters. Once in a while I will take a call from an adjuster if I am not terribly busy. It's usually a twenty-something-year-old high school graduate who wants to tell me about my case, or a sixty-something-year-old who has been drinking the Kool-Aid for thirty years and tries to tell me my sixteen-year-old client has degenerative disc disease and won't vault the verbal threshold.

They explain the law, including facts or evidence they believe a jury will hear despite not knowing the rules of evidence or case law. They even try to explain the medicine. I then ask them what law school they went to. They reply, "Uhhh, I didn't go to law school." Okay then what medical school did they attend? "Uhhh, I didn't go to medical school either." Although I try to keep my cool, I often tell them to not only come to the trial and watch me take all their money, but that when I do, they will be fired. It's kind of a joke around the office, but these adjusters really piss me off.

Now, in the rare instances when we do send settlement packages presuit, we use the same care and packaging as we do with our interrogatories. If there is a limited policy, or the insurance carrier is one that has a history of being reasonable, we may send a settlement package. In the instances where we do send a settlement package it is really just the chronological facts stemming from the negligence of the defendant that will someday be the dominos used at trial.

A more common settlement package we use is the mediation or binding arbitration package. Although these two events typically occur during litigation, there are many cases that warrant mediation presuit. In those instances, a stellar mediation package is mandatory.

If you want to show the defense that you are serious, you must put together a very impressive mediation package. There are places that will prepare them for you, such as the Evidence Store in New Jersey and many other such places across the United States. Or you can create them yourself.

In this package, you must list all of the issues in your case: liability, medical treatment, economic damages, and your demand. The package should have numerous photographs, medical illustrations, time lines, surgery storyboards, and charts and diagrams that lay out economic and future life-care plan figures. The beauty of creating a package like this is that the illustrations you create for the settlement brochure become your trial exhibits in miniature.

I attend mediations and binding arbitrations as if I was going to trial. I bring all my exhibits, have medical and liability experts testify briefly over the telephone, have my clients and conditional witnesses testify live, and even use my dominos to prove proximate cause when the issue may be complex. I know, from the awards that have been rendered in my cases, that the retired judges or attorneys acting as the mediator or arbitrator appreciate all of this hard work.

You can also create video settlement brochures. There are numerous companies that offer this service. When I do create a video brochure, I serve it on the defense and amend interrogatories to include every photo, video, or exhibit contained within the brochure, as the brochure itself will probably not be admissible at trial.

I also use music to accompany the brochure. I saw an attorney from Wisconsin, Jay Urban, at an AAJ Convention in San Francisco demonstrate this. He showed photo clips of a kid who was in a horrific accident and showed him going through his physical therapy, his slow recovery, and then him in the present.

The lawyer claimed he used a video to show the brutal rehab this poor kid had to go through because he had an excellent recovery. He used the band Coldplay's "Fix You" as the background music.

It was amazing. I borrowed that idea from him for a brochure I created for a mediation that took place just three days before a trial. The case settled. However, the insurance company's exposure in that case was tremendous and I had an excellent client with a huge lost-wage claim.

Creating settlement packages may not always get the case settled presuit at the mediation or arbitration, but it does force you to get your exhibits in order prior to the time of trial. If you set up the dominos in the minds of your fact finders and knock them over during your presentation, you can prove the most difficult proximate cause issues in a simple, concise manner. If the case does not settle, this means war!

Chapter Takeaways

- Settlement packages can work on a limited basis, on the right case with severe injuries and limited coverage.

- Create impressive velo-bound settlement packages that include all your surgical storyboards, liability and medical expert reports, and photographs.

- Create your settlement package to mirror what you need for trial to eliminate the need to scramble to get exhibits made at the time of trial.

- Attend mediations and arbitrations as if you are going to trial.

- Use video brochures accompanied by music for emotional impact.

9

THE PRETRIAL EXCHANGE

To believe in something and not to live it, is dishonest.

Mahatma Gandhi

The pretrial exchange is the document you provide to your adversaries and ultimately the judge one week prior to trial. This package contains all the witnesses you will call for trial, your motions *in limine*, the voir dire questions you would like the judge to ask (New Jersey has no lawyer-directed voir dire, only voir dire by the judge. I know it is insane, but it is all we have), and the law that the judge will charge the jury.

There is an attorney in central New Jersey named John Gorman. He is the *in limine* motion king. He has an *in limine* motion for every issue you could think of and is always kind enough to share them with the plaintiff's bar.

I am sure at State Association for Justice seminars, or AAJ Seminars, this topic is covered. If not, the New Jersey Association for Justice (NJAJ) always has plaintiff-only seminars or seminars open to all attorneys where it is covered. I am sure if you contact the NJAJ you can obtain the video of past seminars where this issue was covered. It is extremely important.

In soft-tissue cases, the defense has typical defenses and typical prejudices they play on throughout the case. When the jury sits in the box, they are already against you. Your job, unfortunately, is to not only turn them around 180 degrees so that they rule in your favor, but to turn them around so far that they give your client money.

It is crazy if you think about the hurdles a plaintiff's trial attorney must overcome just to get a fair shake. The cards are stacked against us. To overcome these obstacles, plaintiff's lawyers must be prepared and able to eliminate as many defense tactics as they can. Motions *in limine* can even the playing field. If you can take away all the bullshit defenses they claim in every case, you have a much better shot at being successful.

As I mentioned, the pretrial exchange is a document that should consist of all of the witnesses, trial exhibits, *in limine* motions, evidentiary issues, the verdict sheet, and your proposed jury charges. According to some recent unpublished New Jersey case law, this also requires us to provide all materials we are going to use to cross-examine defense experts, including all prior transcripts.

These transcripts are actually supposed to be exchanged in discovery, but because the case is so recent, I think supplying it at this stage should be acceptable. Combine that with the fact that the defense doctor may be the defense expert in thirty of your cases and these documents must be supplied in discovery in every case. Moreover, if you depose him or cross him in a current case, then you must amend interrogatories in every case in which he is the defense expert.

This task would have been impossible prior to computers these days the documents can be supplied on disc. Although you do have to supply the information you do not have to supply the sections of the transcript you intend to use. This makes sense with regard to trial strategy, but then why supply the thousands of pages you do not intend to use? This practice also flies in the face of the court rules and the art of cross-examination. I am sure some judges will not follow this demanding task if argued correctly at trial or during discovery. But because the bench can be so inconsistent, I am going to take the safe road and supply everything I have.

In New Jersey, through the NJAJ, we have a club called the 50/50 Project. It consists of fifty lawyers who each handle one of the fifty most notorious defense medical experts in the state. The sheer amount of documents accumulated through the 50/50 Project, including trial transcripts, deposition testimony, medical reports, disciplinary reports, websites, news articles, and so on, is voluminous. In some cases, there may be thirty to fifty transcripts on a single defense medical expert and over 4,000 medical reports. This project allows one lawyer to focus on one defense doctor. Every state association should be doing this.

We also have a seminar called "Exposing Deceptive Defense Medicine" every two years and as part of the seminar, we include a package containing all of the materials collected over the course of the two prior years on every defense doctor. I encourage members of every state association to attend to better assist your state in creating and operating your own version of the 50//50 project. When we held the 2015 "Exposing Deceptive Defense Medicine" seminar in Atlantic City, we were fortunate enough to have an amazing faculty that included Rick Friedman from Washington and Dorothy Clay Sims from Florida, as well as some of the best trial lawyers in New Jersey. It was a really special event.

In limine motions are paramount to obtaining a fair trial. When I first began trying cases, I made few, if any, *in limine* motions. I just didn't know any better. All of the prejudicial information regarding prior lawsuits, injuries that were irrelevant, airbags not deploying, and hearsay medical records came in at trial. These days, none of it gets in—because of *in limine* motions. The defense has a script of issues that can destroy your case before you even get started. If you are not doing this in your soft-tissue cases, or any case for that matter, you are making a huge mistake.

You can take away all, if not most, of the usual previously mentioned defenses. Why would a jury need to know that your client had an accident without any injury twenty-five years ago? Why would they need to know your client filed a lawsuit when she was seven-years-old through her parents regarding stitches she received when she fell off her bicycle? Why would they need to know your client's air bag did not deploy when she was rear-ended? Why would they need to know if she saw the lawyer before the doctor? Why would they need to know what some doctor she saw for her shoulder ten years ago wrote in his notes regarding her neck because she had pain radiating into her trapezius and completely unrelated to her recent cervical trauma? Why? Because this is how they defend these cases. They call your client a liar. It is as simple as that.

The amount of anti-lawsuit propaganda that is broadcast to the public is very difficult to overcome. I hear it every day in court when jurors are asked if they have any feelings regarding frivolous lawsuits and they mention the McDonald's coffee case. They mention that doctors are leaving the state because of frivolous malpractice suits. I want to scream. These two examples have been pounded into the heads of the general public and the only counter to these is the documentary *Hot Coffee*, which is excellent, and some sparse, obscure articles stating that statistics show that doctors' malpractice insurance rates are not affected even when there is tort reform and caps on damages.

I know this battle is an uphill one, the political and social climate is getting worse for us trial attorneys, but I am not about to stop trying cases and fighting for my clients. Enough of this pretrial stuff, let's get to the real reason I am writing this book: *the trial*.

Chapter Takeaways

◆ Sending the pretrial exchange documents required by your state sends a message to the defense that you are ready for trial.

◆ Share materials with the plaintiffs' bar in your state. United we stand, divided we fall.

◆ *In limine* motions are essential for weeding out the defense's typical, irrelevant, and prejudicial arguments, and for helping streamline your case for trial.

10

GOING TO TRIAL

I'm in trial mode. It's Black Sabbath all the way to the courthouse.

Edward P. Capozzi

A very skilled defense attorney, who I have tried several cases against, named A. Charles Lorenzo once told me: "A trial against any lawyer is a battle, but a trial against Capozzi is a war."

No words could be more accurate. In fact, I prepare for and try my cases like a war. I treat experts like army tanks, my lay witnesses like soldiers, and I call my office where I prepare for trial the "war room." The defendants are the enemy. The defense attorney is the enemy's general.

I leave my house at four or five a.m. and blast Black Sabbath, Motley Crue, or Alice in Chains all the way to the courthouse where I lie in wait, the first car in the parking lot, planning my attack. Music has always played a great part in my life. I was a musician for twenty years before I went to law school and became a lawyer. Even though I have given up going on stage and performing, music still affects my state of mind. I play Black Sabbath when I am in trial, just like the Army Rangers in *Apocalypse Now* played Wagner's "Ride of the Valkyries" on their way into battle. Obviously a trial is not a war, but for me, this approach works psychologically.

Because I usually cannot sleep, even though I'm exhausted, I often prepare for my witnesses in my car in the parking lot of the courthouse. The sun has not risen; the parking lot attendant has not yet arrived. I wait for *him to open the lot.*

Even when I do sleep, I dream about the trial, the witnesses, and the evidence. I am 100 percent invested in the case. Although I am calm, cordial, and polite in the hallways, I am all business in the courtroom. I am not there to make friends. I am not there to schmooze adjusters. I am there to try the case.

In fact, once I *am* there, I am hardly interested in settling the case. I have my number that can settle the case and I rarely come off it. I feel that when there is good money, but not full value on the case, or an offer that is just enticing enough, I begin to lose my edge. Therefore once I begin the trial, I usually do not budge unless there is a real concern in the case. On the bigger cases, I sometimes bring another lawyer to deal with the adjusters and lawyers while I focus solely on the task at hand: the trial.

I typically have a truckload of exhibits, usually brought to court in boxes by an employee of my office: exhibit bags, easels, markers, models of body parts, electronic equipment, and whatever else I want to use to best explain my case to a jury. I think appearing at court with all of your weapons is a great way to send a message to your adversary that you mean business. When my adversaries do the same thing (and it has only happened once or twice) I definitely know this fellow is ready for action. It has the same psychological effect on my adversaries when I do it. They can try all they want to act cool and collected, but deep down I know they are more concerned than usual.

Speaking of adversaries, although I do not respect the companies they work for, nor the positions they often take in cases, I do understand they are just doing their jobs. They have families, houses to pay for, and for the most part are pretty good people. I often invite defense attorneys to my home for parties. Maybe it's just the old saying: "Keep your friends close and your enemies closer." On the other hand, there are some Kool-Aid drinkers that enjoy what they do and will do anything, at any cost, to deprive our clients of justice. I often go the extra mile to try and teach these guys a lesson.

One thing is certain: without the passion, without the weapons, and without the desire to bring justice to your client, you will not win. These cases are very difficult, and the odds are stacked against us, so we must do everything in our power to level the playing field.

I have read many books on trial work, including *Reptile*, *David Ball on Damages* (all three editions), *Polarizing the Case*, *Rules of the Road*, *Trial by Human*, and many others. When I first read these books, I had already been winning trials, but felt I could always be better. I still feel the same way. You should listen to everyone's ideas and methods to become the best you can be.

One thing I often say at seminars is, "write your own book." Take what you can from everyone else, but be true to yourself. Be yourself and your delivery in court will be sincere and from your heart. Do not try to be someone else; you will appear synthetic.

The funny thing I realized, when I first read these books, is one would say never do this or never do that, and I always did this or always did that—and for me, it worked. The point is to take what you can from the books, but there is no pure way to try a case. The facts are always different and the strategy to try the case must always adapt to those facts and the situation.

My favorite legal book, and favorite all-time lawyer for that matter, is Melvin Belli's *My Life on Trial*. He was the king of demonstrative evidence and a trailblazer in the legal field. He thought outside the box, and he did things no one had ever done before. He is my idol when it comes to trial law. He was also a wild man outside the courtroom, something I have been accused of myself.

After trying my first fifty cases, with more than decent results, I read *Reptile*. I thought the idea was sound and I wanted to incorporate it into my trials. I tried it three times. I lost all three trials. I swore I would never do it again and began to speak out to my colleagues that it does not work. I went back to my own way of trying cases and won ten trials in a row.

However, I saw David Ball lecture recently at an AAJ trucking seminar in New Orleans. He was awesome—like a mad scientist. He stated that the Reptile method has a long learning curve. I wish I had known that before I attempted it. When I tried it, it did not feel natural to me during my opening and I could sense the jury thought I was trying to manipulate them. I was uncomfortable. During the seminar, what he spoke about made great sense, and although I am reluctant to try it again, I may practice it at focus groups and give it another shot.

The domino theory *is* your case. It's the facts of your case placed in chronological order to demonstrate exactly what happened to your client. The trial is the play. You are the director. You control the sequence of your case: the witnesses, the exhibits, and the experts, with the domino theory demonstration as the grand finale. The opening statement is the movie preview. The trial is the movie and the jury verdict is the movie critic's newspaper column critiquing your work, with either a thumb's up: a favorable verdict, or a thumbs down: a no cause.

CHAPTER TAKEAWAYS

◆ Every great attorney I know is an early bird. Wake up early and attack the day, especially when on trial.

◆ Read as many trial books as you can, and take away what tips best suit your personality. Do not force things that work for others on yourself.

◆ Write your own book.

11

Opening Statement

The general who wins the battle makes many calculations in his temple before the battle is fought. The general who loses makes but few calculations beforehand.

Sun Tzu

Being a great trial lawyer is like being a gifted athlete. But instead of playing a single sport like baseball, football, or hockey, you play a different sport every two to four weeks or so, with different rules that you have to learn before the game begins.

Generally, some of the rules are the same, such as the rules of evidence. However, the law of each case is different, the medicine is different, the opponents are different, and the referees are different. Some referees let you play your game; others attempt to limit your arguments and speed through the process, putting efficiency before justice.

This occurs when attorneys are trying to put on their case and an expert's availability becomes an issue. Many judges allow a half-day of testimony if an expert is unavailable, some will not.

Most importantly, the game isn't decided by who scores the most touchdowns. It's decided by six, eight, or twelve strangers who choose which side had the best player.

When I first started practicing law, I had heard that 80 percent of cases were won in opening statement, and I believed it was true. But after trying several dozen cases, I began to believe I was winning my cases in my summation. I thought this because it seemed to me that having the final word gave me the chance to put it all together for the jury without giving the another chance to undo what I had just argued. However, I now believe that opening statement is indeed where cases are won or lost.

Being the first to speak is pivotal. The jury hears the story from you first. If you can persuasively explain the story of your case: the accident, the injuries, the kind of person the plaintiff is, the challenges they have faced from the time of the accident to present day, and the problems they are going to face in the future, then it will be very difficult for the defense to undo what you have set in the jurors' minds. I do a very long opening statement, forty-five minutes to an hour or more if needed. I do not lose a single jurors' attention because I constantly write, draw pictures, and explain the medicine and law through simple analogies and images.

It's not what you say; it's how you say it. The inflection of your voice during crucial testimony and visuals is incredibly important. Take acting classes if you need to; practice your presentation at focus groups, in front of mirrors, anywhere. I also cannot say it enough: visuals, visuals, visuals! When you speak for thirty minutes, the jurors may not remember everything you say. But, if you draw diagrams, charts, and illustrate the relevant law and anatomy—explaining how each works—they will listen and remember.

Give the jury the building blocks that the plaintiff will reinforce in her story. Blocks the doctors will add to when they explain the anatomy, the function of the body parts, what events caused the injury to those body parts, how the injury was caused, how the injury has affected the function of the body parts, and how the body parts will never heal to function in the same way as they did before the accident. In addition, give the jurors a preview of all the testimony and proofs they will hear during the trial. Also discuss the law, and the elements of the law, that you need to prove to win your case.

I learned this from watching criminal cases. Prosecutors often break down the law. They tell the jury what the elements of the crime the defendant is being charged with are, and that they need to prove each and every element. They also state how they are going to prove each and every element of their case beyond a reasonable doubt.

In civil law, the plaintiff *is* the prosecutor. The plaintiff has the burden of proof, and just like a prosecutor, has elements that she needs to prove in order to prevail. I find it is crucial during opening statement to explain to the jurors why they are here and what they need to focus on during the course of the trial. I write out the elements of my client's case and what the evidence will show that proves my client's case. I then explain to the jury what evidence the defense will show and try to explain to them why that evidence is incorrect.

It is not easy to explain what will happen without arguing the facts of your case. However, if you break it down and are careful, you can present your case without actually arguing it. I have had many objections during my opening statements, and sometimes they are sustained and sometimes they are not. I am not telling you to disregard the general rule that the opening statement is not argument. I am only telling you it can be done with actual argument with the correct precursors like the old, "evidence and testimony will show."

I have watched many trials on Court TV, in actual courtrooms, on television, and in movies. I have also heard jurors speak about their trial experiences after a trial. I have heard what they like and do not like. In one such experience, a juror stated he did not like me shuffling papers, even though I felt I was hardly shuffling papers at all.

One thing I learned from that juror, and cannot stress enough, is to be organized. If you are going to use notes, and I strongly suggest you do not, then make a clear outline in large letters you can see from where you are standing during your opening, only glancing at it when you need to. Do not carry pages of scribbled notes and read off of the pages. I have gotten to the point in my career where I do not use notes of any kind, probably because that juror told me I shuffled too many papers. Following that experience, I forced myself to learn my cases even colder than I had previously thought necessary.

I use the same format for my opening statement outline (which is what we'll be covering in the next several chapters) for every case. I know it by heart and can fit the facts of every case into its structure. This way, I can execute my opening statements without reading from a single sheet of paper.

I strongly suggest each and every lawyer learn their cases well enough so that they have them completely memorized. It is a lot of information, but if you know your case cold, you'll not only be able to recall the dates without the need of your notes, you'll remember the findings of the diagnostic tests and the physical examination as well. The jury is used to seeing lawyers on television and in the movies, where they never use notes. They will expect the same from you. Below is part of an opening statement I gave in a recent trial:

> When you drive the streets and highways of New Jersey, you have to watch where you are going, because if you do not and harm comes to someone, you are responsible for that harm. We drive our vehicles within inches of each other at high speeds, only painted lines separating us. We have traffic signals, stop signs, yield signs, no U-turn signs, speed limits—in other words,

we have rules of the road. We all learned those rules when we took our written driver's test and later our road test. We have expectations that each and every one of us will obey those signs and those rules.

We trust one another. It is very dangerous if someone does not. However, when one of these drivers (and it happens every day) fails to obey the traffic signs and the rules of the road, family members, friends, people get injured, even killed.

Evidence and testimony will show that on February 27, 2009, the defendant left her home to go to work. She had to be there at 8 a.m. She pulled out of her driveway, turned left on McKinley Street and then left on Dwight Street. As she approached the intersection of Main Street, she stopped at the stop sign, looked briefly right and began her left turn.

That same morning, Jessica Amada left her home around 7:45 a.m. and was heading to school. She was a sophomore at Rutgers University. She left her parents' driveway, turned onto Plane Street and then made a right onto Main Street. Main Street is a two-lane street, one lane in each direction. She was traveling 30 mph, even slower than the 35 mph posted speed limit, when all of a sudden a vehicle pulled out of Dwight Street directly in front of her. It was the defendant.

She tried to avoid the accident, but there was oncoming traffic coming towards her so she could only slam on the brakes. It wasn't enough. There was a loud bang, glass, metal, and plastic flew everywhere and the air bag exploded into her face. She will tell you that she was thrown forward and back and side to side like a rag doll. Luckily her seat belt held her body in place, but the tremendous impact caused her neck to hyper extend. There is no seatbelt for your neck.

Evidence and testimony will show that when she realized what had just happened, she felt like it was a dream. The dust from the air bag was raining down on her, she had abrasions on her face where the air bag struck her, and she felt a sharp pain in her neck. People began running over to her and asking if she was all right. She was crying and pleading with people to get her out of the car. They could not open her driver's door. A man opened her passenger door, but was afraid to move her due to her injuries and just tried to calm her down before the police arrived.

As you can see, this is straight out of *Rules of the Road*.[1] However, I also actively engage the jury by drawing the accident scene for them while I describe it.

CHAPTER TAKEAWAYS

- In opening statement, lay out the Rules of the Road the defendant violated.

- Teach the jury the elements you need to prove so they can focus their attention on the law.

- Tell the jury the facts of your case and precisely what occurred to your client.

- Keep the attention of the jury by drawing or using images, words alone are not enough.

1 Rick Friedman and Patrick Malone, *Rules of the Road*, 2nd ed. (Portland: Trial Guides, 2010).

12

DISCUSSING THE ACCIDENT AND TREATMENT IN OPENING STATEMENT

Americans love to fight. All real Americans love the sting of battle.

General George S. Patton

I start speaking immediately when I stand to begin my opening and walk over to the easel. I do not thank the jurors for performing their civic duty, nor do I thank them for serving on this jury. I am all business.

I begin to draw the accident scene as I speak. I know many lawyers cannot draw, but I use a simple diagram of the scene and even the least artistic lawyer should be able to draw a traffic intersection. I also use magnetic boards and cars depicting aerial views of the scene.[1] However, there is a downside to the boards; the cars get moved throughout the trial by various witnesses, and I like the permanency of the actual drawing to refer to in my closing. Although the combination of the aerial view and magnetic cars is an excellent feature during trial, I like to draw the accident scene as well.

THE ACCIDENT

I begin my opening using the Rules of the Road™ premise that, "if you drive the roads and highways of New Jersey you have to watch where you're going and follow the rules of the road, because if you don't and you cause harm to someone, you are responsible for that harm." I then begin to draw the accident scene and explain what the evidence and testimony will show. As I tell the story of the accident, I add in the features of the scene as I explain each fact.

The diagram above is the final product of what I am about to explain. I draw in the streets, cars, and traffic signs as I say the following:

> This case is about an automobile accident. Evidence and testimony will show that on April 27, 2007, at about 8 a.m., Ms. Jones was driving to work on Smith Street in Ridgewood, NJ. Evidence will show that Smith Street is a two-lane road (one lane in each direction) that intersects with Adams Lane, a one-way street controlled by a stop sign. Evidence and testimony will show that the defendant was coming up Adams Lane and instead of stopping and looking both ways before proceeding, glanced to her left, and continued through the intersection, never seeing the

1 As mentioned in chapter 6

vehicle driven by Mrs. Jones, and ultimately colliding with Ms. Jones' vehicle.

That's correct, at the accident scene, the defendant told the police office that she never saw Ms. Jones' car. Ms. Jones told the police officer that the defendant's vehicle never came to a complete stop before entering the intersection and striking her vehicle. She also told him that she tried to avoid the collision but there was oncoming traffic heading towards her, and although she applied her brakes, it was too late to stop. You will hear from Officer Washington, who responded to the scene, and he will testify to what I just told you, including where the vehicles impacted (POI), where the debris field was, and where the vehicles came to rest. He will also tell you about Mrs. Jones' complaints of pain at the scene, and that an ambulance arrived, treated her briefly, and rushed her to the hospital. He will also tell you about the damage to the vehicles and that they were both towed from the scene.

After I complete the accident scene diagram, I move right onto what happened after the accident. I begin with the medical treatment Mrs. Jones received, including that she immediately experienced an onset of pain. This is an important element to the domino theory and it pinpoints when the disc probably herniated because the pain was immediate. I know every case does not have this convenient fact so if there is not the immediate onset of pain, make sure you cover this important topic with your medical expert.

It is not uncommon for someone who was just involved in an automobile accident to not feel anything at the scene. They are shaken up, adrenaline is flowing, and soft-tissue injuries are inflammable by nature and typically worsen over the forty-eight hours following the trauma. I use going to the gym or what NFL players experience following a football game as an analogy.

With regard to my own experience working out, I explain that when someone goes to the gym for the first time in a long time, he does not feel any pain while he's working out and tearing and stretching the muscle fibers in his body. But the next day, and especially the second day after, he cannot move. He's extremely sore. Every muscle he worked out hurts.

With regard to football players, they crash into each other at high speeds with tremendous force. These are world-class athletes. It is no surprise that following a Sunday football game, there is no practice for two days because the players are sitting in whirl pools and being seen by trainers to address all of the ailments they suffered from the game one or two days prior.

There are many ways to explain to a jury why there was not an immediate onset of pain, and the doctors can discuss this with the jury while they are testifying. The lack of the immediate onset of pain is one of the handful of defense excuses for non-injury following an automobile accident, so be sure to prepare for it through your client's testimony and through expert medical testimony.

Additionally, make sure you cover your client's complaints at the emergency room and at the presentation of all her treating doctors. It is not uncommon for a client to state at her deposition that she complained of neck and back pain at the emergency room when in fact she did not. If you broke your arm it is probably what your chief complaint was at the hospital, even if you injured your neck and back as well.

Hopefully there is a CT scan or X-ray of your client's neck or back at the emergency department. Even if there were no complaints at the time of triage, the emergency department doctor usually does a physical exam and diagrams the patient's complaints. Inconsistencies in the medical records are another way the defense typically defends these types of cases. Be sure to move *in limine* to exclude any information that is not given to the emergency room staff for the purpose of treatment. I am often successful in keeping out phrases like "low impact," "minor property damage," and "head-on collision" as they are often inaccurate and can derail your case before you even get started. The treatment that follows the defendant's negligence and the collision can really tighten up your proximate cause argument. It is extremely important to proving your case.

THE TREATMENT

After I explain how the accident occurred, I begin to write out the treatment my client underwent after the collision. When I explain the accident and then immediately detail my client's treatment for the jury, they're hearing a spontaneous and continuous sequence of events for the first time. They hear about the accident, the immediate onset of pain, whether the airbag deployed, the ambulance ride, the emergency room visit, and then about the first doctor's appointment following the initial accident. I continue by outlining the treatment in chronological order: the chiropractor visit, the MRI, the neurology consult, the EMG, the findings of these diagnostic tests, the continued pain, the pain management, the epidurals, and either the ultimate surgery or continued pain without surgery. These are the building blocks of the domino theory for a soft-tissue personal injury case.

Treatment Timeline

April 27, 2007 — Motor vehicle collision

April 27, 2007 — Emergency room: Memorial Hospital (reversal of the lordotic curve of the cervical spine)

April 29, 2007 — Dr. Berger, PCP: spasm

May 1, 2007 — Dr. Lee, chiropractor: three times a week for twelve weeks (spasm)

July 1, 2007 — MRI of the cervical spine: C5-C6 HNP, MRI of the lumbar spine: L4-5 bulge, L5-S1 HNP

July 5, 2007 — Dr. Maggiano, neurologist: initial evaluation (spasm)

July 10, 2007 — EMG with Dr. Maggiano: C5 radiculopathy, L5 radiculopathy

July 27, 2007 — Dr. Vesper, orthopedist: initial consult (spasm)

July 30, 2007 — Physical therapy three times a week for four weeks

August 4, 2007 — Last chiropractic visit (fifty-seven visits total with spasm)

September 1, 2007 — Dr. James: initial consultation for pain management (spasm and diminished reflex)

September 14, 2007 — Cervical epidural (fluoroscopy)

September 30, 2007 — Cervical epidural (fluoroscopy)

October 20, 2007 — Cervical epidural (fluoroscopy)

January 12, 2008 — Lumber epidural (fluoroscopy)

January 30, 2008 — Lumbar epidural (fluoroscopy)

February 19, 2008 — Lumbar epidural (fluoroscopy)

April 14, 2008 — Discogram of the lumbar spine: positive at L4-L5 (fluoroscopy)

April 14, 2008 — Post discogram CT scan of the lumbar spine: bulge with annular tear at L4-L5, L5-S1 HNP

May 1, 2008 — Medial branch block at L4-L5 (fluoroscopy)

May 30, 2008 — Intradiscal electrothermal annuloplasty (IDET): L4-L5 Lumbar spine (fluoroscopy)

June 15, 2008 — Discogram of the cervical spine: positive at C5-C6 (fluoroscopy)

June 15, 2008 — Post discogram CT scan of the cervical spine: C5-C6 HNP

July 17, 2008 — Orthopedic visit: physical therapy three times a week for eight weeks

December 12, 2008 — Last PT visit

January 28, 2009 — Defense exam with Dr. Blood, neurologist: no spasm or objective evidence of permanent injury

January 31, 2009 — Follow up visit with Dr. Maggiano, neurologist: spasm

February 14, 2009 — Defense exam with Dr. Wurst, orthopedist: no spasm or objective evidence of permanent injury

February 22, 2009 — Follow up with Dr. James, orthopedist: spasm, limited ROM cervical and lumbar spine

March 1, 2010 — Today

This is the first time the domino theory will be laid out before the jury—but subliminally. I do not mention the domino theory. This will come later in my opening, during my explanation of the proximate cause of the injuries. I will use this handwritten chronology of events during the direct examination of my client, the direct examination of my medical experts, the cross-examination of the defense medical experts, and during my closing argument to show not only the continuous sequence of events (which is the domino theory), but also to prove the injuries through objective medical evidence. Regarding objective evidence: I mention the doctors' findings that were objective either on exam or through diagnostic testing. This sets up the objective medical evidence standard that the defense often states is absent. When I cross-examine a defense expert, the argument becomes ridiculous when I point out to him each and every objective finding in the three years after the accident. This is how I lay out the dominos in the minds of the jurors, beginning with the accident and continuing chronologically with the treatment.

Chapter Twelve Takeaways

- Draw out the accident scene to familiarize the jury with the scene. If you only talk about it without showing it, it will be difficult for the jury to grasp what you are saying regardless of how clear you think it sounds.

- Chronologically explain the events leading up to the collision including what occurred to your client inside the vehicle.

- Chronologically describe the medical treatment to subliminally lay out the dominos.

- Writing out the medical treatment in chronological order allows you to use this exhibit throughout the trial on the direct and cross of medical experts.

13

THE ELEMENTS

Carry the battle to them. Don't let them bring it to you. Put them on the defensive and don't ever apologize for anything.

President Harry S. Truman

During my opening statement, I explain the four elements the plaintiff must prove in order to obtain a verdict and recover damages in an automobile negligence case. I write these four elements on the board and discuss each one:[1]

1. THE △ WAS _____ NEGLIGENT.

2. THE △'S NEGLIGENCE WAS _____ A PROXIMATE CAUSE OF THE ACCIDENT.

3. THE △'S NEGLIGENCE WAS _____ A PROXIMATE CAUSE OF THE INJURIES.

4. THE INJURIES ARE _____ PERMANENT.

---

1 I use the delta symbol in this example because I often like to use different terms such as "driver" or "defendant," depending on which seems most appropriate.

THE DEFENDANT WAS NEGLIGENT

In a non-rear-end automobile accident, the defense typically does not stipulate to liability. Instead, they attempt to create some percentage of liability that is the plaintiff's fault. They usually argue that the plaintiff could have attempted to avoid the accident in some way (by either braking or swerving), that the plaintiff was speeding, or that the plaintiff was not observant prior to the accident. These issues must be worked out before depositions to avoid uncertain or poor testimony being used at trial. Surprisingly, this defense tactic is quite persuasive and can impact the amount of the plaintiff's verdict. You must prepare for this issue from the start of the case.

While explaining to the jury what negligence is, be careful not to violate the judge's domain. The judge will instruct the jury what the actual law is after all the testimony has been presented. I typically say something like "negligence is basically someone acting unreasonably." I then say that the judge is going to define negligence when she charges the jury, but for the purpose of what I need to prove: negligence is an unreasonable act or omission. I further tell them that if my representation of the law differs from what the judge tells them later, then they must follow the law as instructed by the judge and disregard my explanation.

I have heard the law charged so many times, my version of it is identical to the judges, so I never worry that it will differ. In fact, I attempt to mimic the jury charges verbatim as often as I can during the trial to familiarize the jury with the concepts of the law. Naturally, the more they hear it—and hear it from me—the more credibility I will have with the jury when the judge reads them the jury charges and they are identical to what I have been saying throughout the trial. In New Jersey, the state that I practice in, negligence is defined as:

> *Negligence* may be defined as a failure to exercise, in the given circumstances, that degree of care for the safety of others, which a person of ordinary prudence

would exercise under similar circumstances. It may be the doing of an act which the ordinary prudent person would not have done, or the failure to do that which the ordinary prudent person would have done, under the circumstances then existing.[2]

Where a more detailed definition is desired, the following may be used:

> *Negligence* is the failure to use that degree of care, precaution and vigilance which a reasonably prudent person would use under the same or similar circumstances. It includes both affirmative acts which a reasonably prudent person would not have done and the omission of acts or precautions which a reasonably prudent person would have done or taken in the circumstances.
>
> By "a reasonably prudent person" it is not meant the most cautious person nor one who is unusually bold but rather one of reasonable vigilance, caution, and prudence.
>
> In order to establish negligence, it is not necessary that it be shown that the defendant had an evil heart or an intent to do harm.
>
> To summarize, every person is required to exercise the foresight, prudence, and caution which a reasonably prudent person would exercise under the same or similar circumstances. Negligence then is a departure from that standard of care.[3]

---

2 New Jersey Model Civil Jury Charges, available at http://www.judiciary. state.nj.us/civil/civindx.htm

3 Ibid.

Every state has its own definition of negligence that can be found in its model jury charges. This should either be on the state court's website or in texts on causes of action from your individual state.

In my opening statement, I tell the jury that the plaintiff has the burden of proof to prove these four elements. I direct them to element number one and write the following:

1. THE △ WAS _____ NEGLIGENT.

I then begin to explain to the jury what the driver did that was negligent. For example, I might say something like: "In this case, the defendant admitted that she never saw Mrs. Jones. She only briefly looked left before entering the intersection. It is as simple as that. This is what she told the police at the scene, what she told me at her deposition, and what she will tell all of you at this trial."

Most jurors are familiar with the rules of driving and can easily figure out who was at fault for an accident. When the defense stipulates to liability, I explain to the jury that the defendant's negligence was a proximate cause of the accident, and the first and the second elements are met because the defendant admits both of them. In that situation, all Mrs. Jones must prove are elements three and four. However, I still discuss the defendant's negligence and describe the impact of the collision because I still need to prove my client's injuries and it helps to explain what the defendant did and what happened to my client.

THE DEFENDANT'S NEGLIGENCE WAS A PROXIMATE CAUSE OF THE ACCIDENT

The second element the plaintiff has to prove is that the defendant's negligence was a proximate cause of the accident. I write it out for the jury as follows:

2. THE △'S NEGLIGENCE WAS _____
A PROXIMATE CAUSE OF THE ACCIDENT.

I tell them the defendant admitted she never saw the plaintiff. She only glanced to the left prior to entering the intersection. If she had completely stopped and surveyed the traffic conditions, the accident would never have occurred. Thus, her negligence—failing to act reasonably and stop before entering the intersection—caused the accident. I remind them that if she had stopped and looked both ways carefully and reasonably, the accident would never have happened, Mrs. Jones would never have been injured, and we'd never have met.

In fact, I tell them that Mrs. Jones would have driven past the intersection, continued on her way, and arrived safely at work. She wouldn't have been involved in a collision, injured, or taken to the emergency room by ambulance, and this lawsuit would never have arisen. I begin to lay the foundation for the domino theory. But for the defendant's negligence, the accident does not happen and the events that followed do not happen. And now the first three or four dominos have been placed in the minds of the jury.

It's common for a defendant to stipulate to liability in a rear-end collision or any other obvious case. If this happens, I explain to the jury that the defendant has admitted that not only were they negligent, but that they also caused the accident. I then place an X after elements one and two, because they were already proven by the defendant's stipulation of fault.

1. THE △ WAS NEGLIGENT. X

2. THE △'S NEGLIGENCE WAS A PROXIMATE CAUSE OF THE ACCIDENT. X

THE DEFENDANT'S NEGLIGENCE WAS A PROXIMATE CAUSE OF THE INJURIES

The next element the plaintiff has to prove is that the defendant's negligence was a proximate cause of the injuries. Again, I write out the third element of the plaintiff's case.

> 3. THE △'S NEGLIGENCE WAS _____
> A PROXIMATE CAUSE OF THE INJURIES.

I emphasize that this is what the trial is all about. I remind the jury that the defendant admitted she never saw the plaintiff and only glanced left prior to entering the intersection. I remind them that if the defendant had completely stopped and surveyed the traffic conditions prior to entering the intersection, the accident would never have occurred, and Mrs. Jones would not have been injured. Thus, the defendant's negligence—her failure to act reasonably and stop and carefully look both ways before entering the intersection—set in motion a series of events that led to the accident and Mrs. Jones's injuries. Thus, her negligence proximately caused this accident and my client's injuries.

Now we have the key domino in the series of events: *negligence*. Negligence is the key domino because it sets all of the other dominos in motion to fall.

Since the cause of my client's injuries is typically what is defended the fiercest, I spend extra time on their causation and explain to the jury that this is what the case is *all* about. I argue that but for the defendant's negligence and the accident, Mrs. Jones's air bag would not have deployed—striking her in the face. Her neck would not have hyper extended, her knee would not have struck the dashboard, her seatbelt would not have restricted her left shoulder (drivers typically injure their left shoulder because the harness restricts left shoulder movement while front seat passengers typically injure their right), and she would not have gone to the hospital and seen all the doctors she had to see and will probably be following up with for the rest of her life. I then go on to list the injuries she is claiming:

- A herniated disc of the C5-C6 level of her cervical spine

- A torn meniscus in her right knee

- A torn rotator cuff in her left shoulder

I further say that I will "discuss the injuries in a moment, but let's discuss the causation of the injuries for now." I draw a timeline of my client's life beginning with birth. In linear fashion, I include the years before her accident, the day of the accident, and then the treatment I outlined in the earlier part of my opening.

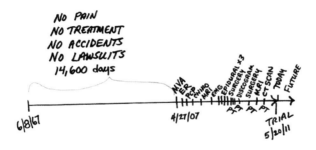

Hand Drawn Example: Client Timeline

I then explain that Mrs. Jones was born on June 8, 1967, graduated from high school in 1985, and graduated from college in 1989 (I do not write this as I want to focus on as little information about events prior to the accident as possible). Then I write the date of the accident and all of the treatment following it, beginning with April 27, 2007. There is an obvious thirty-year gap before we get to the accident date and then a very crowded timeline thereafter that shows all of the treatment she received, as well as the diagnoses connected with the accident.

The timeline clearly indicates that something occurred on April 27, 2007 that necessitated all of the treatment and undoubtedly caused the injuries. The absence of any treatment prior to this accident further establishes the ridiculousness of the defense's argument that the injuries were preexisting. I point out that prior to April 27, 2007, Mrs. Jones never saw a doctor for her neck, knee, or shoulder; never experienced pain in her neck, knee, or shoulder; never was in another auto accident, fall-down accident, work accident, or injured herself playing sports; and she had never filed a lawsuit of any kind.

She was perfectly healthy and, but for seeing her primary care physician for routine check-ups, had not seen a doctor for any reason. In fact, her primary care doctor's records dating back to 1991 do not reflect a single complaint of knee, neck, or shoulder pain. This is so important.

I often tell my paralegals to "get the client's PCP records."

They respond by saying, "but they did not treat with their PCP for this accident."

I say, "no kidding, get me the records so I can show that the client has never before complained of pain in the affected areas that she now claims are injured. And get them as far back as they go." This practice can also flush out any prior problems your client swears didn't exist before the accident. Either way, you need this important information to help prove your case and be prepared for the defense argument that she had prior complaints to these areas of the body.

Causation is the easiest to explain using the domino theory. Surprisingly, most plaintiff's attorneys do not realize that, regardless if the case is a limitation of lawsuit case or not, the defense doctors always take the preexisting, "not causally related" stance to defend the case. They will typically give you permanency, but they'll state that the injury, although permanent, was preexisting.

Thus, I explain to the jury that permanency is *not* the issue. Every doctor will agree that a herniated disc is permanent. The issue is about element number three: causation of injury.

THE INJURIES ARE PERMANENT

When I discuss my client's injuries with the jury, I draw medical illustrations and educate the jury on the injuries and body parts the medical experts will later discuss. But first I direct them to the fourth and final element needed to prove a plaintiff's personal injury automobile case.

4. THE INJURIES ARE _____ PERMANENT

Although the spine, knees, and shoulders may be familiar to us attorneys, the jury (for the most part) has most likely never dealt with injuries to these body parts and they need to be taught about them in an easy, show-and-tell like fashion. I teach the jury about the anatomy and explain that they will hear from various physicians who will teach them about the anatomy and function of the body parts affected in this case.

If the body part or organ will not function normally again, even with further medical treatment, then the injury is considered permanent. This is the definition I must work with in the State of New Jersey.

When a disc herniates, a knee tendon or ligament or cartilage tears, or a shoulder tendon or muscle tears, they heal with fibrous scar tissue, if at all. Scar tissue is not as elastic as normal tissue. Discs have a very poor blood supply and never heal. They begin to rapidly *desiccate* or dry out, the disc space diminishes or narrows, the shock absorber function of the disc is lost, and the nerve roots begin to become impinged.

With regard to spinal disc injuries and proving your case, permanency is the easiest of the elements to prove. In New Jersey, the legal definition of permanency is that the body part or organ has not healed to function normally, and will not heal to function normally even with further treatment. The disc, as it relates to the spine, has four functions:

1. A spacer

2. A flexor

3. A shock absorber

4. A connector

As I will explain, bulging or herniation affects all of the disc's four functions. A bulge is an outward swelling of the disc caused by small tears and a shift of the nucleus towards the outer wall of the annulus. A herniation is a complete tear of the annulus that allows the nucleus to leak out through the tear and usually appears as a focal or fingerlike projection.

> **Function 1:** A spacer: One function of the spinal disc is to act as a spacer between the vertebrae above and below. This space allows the nerve roots to exit through the neural foramina, or openings. When a disc bulges or herniates, the disc height decreases and thus the space between the vertebrae narrows, making it more difficult for the nerves to exit through the foramen and sometimes even pinches or compresses the nerve root. In time, the disc will start to dry out, and even thin out, making the space between the vertebrae even smaller. Thus, the spacer function of the disc will be compromised.

> **Function 2:** A flexor: Another function of the spinal disc is to allow the spine to flex forward and backward and side-to-side. The human spine has twenty-four to twenty-six spinal discs. Each disc, being somewhat flexible, allows the spine to flex in various directions at all levels of the spinal column. However, once a disc herniates or bulges, it begins to dry out, or desiccate, and the spine loses its elasticity or ability to bend and flex optimally.

Function 3: A shock absorber: The most well known function of the disc is as a shock absorber. The buoyancy of the discs allows the disc to absorb the load of our bodies and act as a shock absorber to absorb the stress of the weight when we walk, run or jump. When a disc bulges or herniates, the disc dries out, or desiccates, and common sense tells us the disc will then not function in the capacity to absorb weight and impact.

Function 4: A connector: A healthy disc tightly connects the bones above and below preventing shifting and retrolisthesis. When the annulus stretches or tears, allowing a disc to bulge or herniate, the disc becomes less taut and less stable, allowing the vertebrae to shift to and fro.

There is not a doctor on earth who will not admit that a bulging or herniated spinal disc will function normally again. They may attempt to insinuate that the person, as a whole, may function normally again, including carrying out all their daily functions, but that is not the legal definition in New Jersey. The legal definition of permanency as it relates to a spinal injury in an automobile case in New Jersey is:

In this case, the plaintiff alleges that [*he*] [*she*] suffered a permanent injury as a result of the motor vehicle accident. An injury shall be considered permanent when the body part or organ, or both, has not healed to function normally and will not heal to function normally with further medical treatment.

Plaintiff must prove this claim through objective, credible medical evidence. Objective proof means the injury must be verified by physical examination or medical testing and cannot be based solely upon the plaintiff's subjective complaints. Credible evidence is evidence you find to be believable.[4]

A common defense physician tactic is to claim that the disc herniation will re-absorb itself over time. This creates a false impression with the jury that a disc herniation is not permanent or that it heals itself. However, the fact that the herniated disc material may dissolve or be re-absorbed back into the body of the disc does not change the fact that the annulus of the disc is torn completely through and will actually dry out at a faster rate, leading to a compromise of all the functions listed above. I have cross-examined many defense doctors who have attempted this tactic and below is an example from an actual trial where a defense orthopedist attempts to claim a herniated disc is not permanent and will resolve itself whether treated or untreated.

Cross-Examination of a Defense Orthopedist

Q: A herniation is permanent, right?

A: No, it can resolve.

Q: Oh yeah, what percentage is that?

A: I don't know.

Q: You don't know?

A: I don't...

Q: Is it more probable it will resolve or not?

---

4 New Jersey Model Civil Jury Charges, available at: http://www.judiciary. state.nj.us/civil/civindex.htm

A: I don't know.

Q: Then doctor, how do you, what are you talking about? Why are you testifying that it is not permanent?

A: That's not what I said.

Q: Is a disc herniation permanent?

A: If a person has a herniated disc, that disc is injured and will not heal back to the way it was before the injury.

Q: Okay?

A: Can the herniation resolve with or without treatment? Yes.

Q: What do you mean the herniation can resolve? Are you talking about pathology or symptomatology?

A: Both. Most of the time the symptoms go away. The disc herniation, which is the piece of disc material out of place, treated or untreated, will frequently shrink down and sometimes go away.

Q: And the disc will function as if it was never herniated?

A: No, I didn't say that.

Q: Well, then is it permanent or not? Will the disc function normally again after it's herniated?

A: Like I said, no. It doesn't return to what it was before.

Q: Exactly. So it's a permanent injury, right?

A: Yes.

That is a prime example of why understanding the medicine is mandatory in being able to cross-examine medical experts. If you truly understand the medicine, a doctor cannot misrepresent the medicine without being caught. Most lawyers know very little about the medicine that is at the very heart of their case.

Defense lawyers are no different. They know a few questions to ask and little more. I often tell my medical experts at trial, "You are the doctor, he is a lawyer. Do not let this guy push you around. He doesn't know anything other than, 'isn't it true degeneration can cause a herniation?' Smack him down. If you tried to cross-examine me on the law, I would crush you. Do the same exact thing to him." One caveat: some defense lawyers do know the medicine, but even then, the medicine is on our side not theirs. The case boils down to the timeline and the history of the client. If someone has not experienced back pain in over 10,000 days and it begins after the collision, nothing can explain it other than they were injured due to that collision.

Defense doctors typically do not know legal definitions such as the one for "permanency." Ask them what they mean by something being permanent. I have heard some bizarre answers from, "something that lasts forever," to "something that lasts more than fifteen years." When I heard that answer, I asked the doctor if we should adjourn the trial for fifteen years and come back to see if my client was permanently injured. During your cross-examination, set them up by breaking down the legal definition without them knowing it. They will often concede that your client's injury meets the legal definition without even realizing that they have just proven your case.

Another legal definition that doctors have difficulty with is "a reasonable degree of medical probability." I often prepare my doctors for that definition and I always ask the defense doctor if he even knows what a "reasonable degree of medical probability" is. Amazingly, they often have no idea. They do not even know what they are testifying to. Try it, you will see. One defense doctor told me, "something within the realm of reality." I had fun with that one. So, make sure your doctors are prepared for these types of questions and make sure you always ask the defense medical doctor the medical *and* legal definitions that are involved in your case.

So now that you have explained to the jury the four elements needed to prove a soft-tissue case, you must next teach them the standard of proof.

Chapter Thirteen Takeaways

- Explain each element of the law you need to prove and that it is your burden of proof.

- Leave a blank space to insert the standard of proof.

- Describe the law accurately and inform the jury this is the judge's domain and if anything you say is different than what the judge tells them then they must follow the judge's instructions.

- Familiarize the jury with the medicine and explain the medicine to the jury in the context of "this is what the doctors will tell you."

- Use basic repetition teaching. The more they hear it, the more they will understand it.

- Do not let the defense expert get off the hook. If he is deceptive, corner him.

14

A PREPONDERANCE OF THE EVIDENCE

The probability that we may fail in the struggle ought not to deter us from the support of a cause we believe to be just.

President Abraham Lincoln

The "preponderance of the evidence" standard is a low one. Explain to the jury that the standard is not "beyond a reasonable doubt," like they see on television shows like *Law and Order* or *CSI*, but a lesser one. I tell them that those are criminal cases on TV; this is a civil case. It's 51–49 percent. The standard they have to follow is what is more *probable*, what is more likely.

I like to use the O. J. Simpson trials as an example of the difference between "preponderance of the evidence" and "beyond a reasonable doubt." In the criminal trial of O. J. Simpson, the prosecution could not prove that he was guilty beyond a reasonable doubt. The defense had put reasonable doubt in the jurors' minds because of alleged police misconduct and poorly collected DNA samples. O. J. was found not guilty. However at the subsequent civil trial, a different jury concluded, using the preponderance of the evidence standard, that O. J. had *probably* murdered Mrs. Simpson and Mr. Goldman and awarded their families $33 million dollars.

I explain to the jury that after the evidence is in, they will have to decide what probably happened. Which story was more likely, the story presented by the plaintiff or the story that the defense presented? When viewed in this light, the defense story can be portrayed not only as less probable, or as a coincidence, but in fact as quite ridiculous.

GO BACK TO THE FOUR ELEMENTS

After explaining to the jury that the standard of proof is "what probably happened," I go back to the four elements that I need to prove:

1. THE △ WAS _____ NEGLIGENT.

2. THE △'S NEGLIGENCE WAS _____ A PROXIMATE CAUSE OF THE ACCIDENT.

3. THE △'S NEGLIGENCE WAS _____ A PROXIMATE CAUSE OF THE INJURIES.

4. THE INJURIES ARE _____ PERMANENT.

Insert the Word "Probably" into Each Element

Then I go through and insert the word "probably" into each element:

1. THE △ WAS *PROBABLY* NEGLIGENT.

2. THE △'S NEGLIGENCE WAS *PROBABLY* A PROXIMATE CAUSE OF THE ACCIDENT.

3. THE △'S NEGLIGENCE WAS *PROBABLY* A PROXIMATE CAUSE OF THE INJURIES.

4. THE INJURIES ARE *PROBABLY* PERMANENT.

I have now made the case much easier to prove. The preponderance of the evidence standard is not a high hurdle to overcome.

However, you must be careful not to make it sound to the jury that your case is weak but you can still win because the standard of proof is low. Tell the jury that not only are you going to prove this case by a preponderance of the evidence, but that you will prove it beyond a reasonable doubt—or any doubt. It is a simple case, with no other explanation, except for a ridiculous argument by the defense that your client's injuries were preexisting.

Your client's medical history will easily debunk any argument by the defense and their crooked doctors that he had degenerative changes, wherever his injuries are. If it is a neck injury, they'll argue that your client has preexisting degenerative disc disease. If it is a shoulder injury, then there was a preexisting degenerative tear present. If it is a knee injury, there was arthritis and degenerative changes in the cartilage of the knee. If there is a fractured femur, they had osteoarthritis and osteoporosis. In a vacuum, this line of argument from the defense can tend to be problematic.

However, if you can show the jury through cross-examining the defense doctor that this is the identical argument he has given in every case he has ever reviewed—and in fact he has never found a single patient he examined to be injured—debunking this kind of argument is a much easier task to accomplish. When combined with your client's medical history and their treating doctors' testimony, it should make your case a winner—if presented correctly.

It is important to understand that you are not arguing *the* proximate cause; you are arguing *a* proximate cause. A proximate cause is a cause that is a substantial factor in bringing about the accident and the injuries. There can also be other causes. When you clarify this for the jury it makes it easier for them to understand and give your client a just verdict.

Chapter Takeaways

◆ You must explain to the jury that the standard of proof is a "preponderance of the evidence."

◆ Explain to the jury that "preponderance of the evidence" is different than the "beyond a reasonable doubt" standard, with which they are much more familiar.

◆ You must explain to the jury that the definition of pre-ponderance of the evidence means "probably or more likely than not."

◆ Repeat this standard repeatedly throughout the trial to embed it in the jurors' minds.

15

COMMON
SOFT-TISSUE INJURIES

Wherever the art of medicine is loved, there is also a love of humanity.

Hippocrates

The majority of injuries suffered in automobile accidents are primarily soft-tissue injuries to the neck and back. These are also the most difficult injuries to prove at trial. Knee, shoulder, and jaw injuries are also common, but not as much as neck and back injuries. The reason neck and back injuries are so difficult to prove is two-fold.

First, there is so much negative propaganda generated by the insurance defense bar that the public's, or jurors', perception is so skewed against us it is extremely difficult to convince them that our clients' injuries are real. There are television commercials, radio commercials, billboards, and newspaper stories regarding insurance fraud and its effect on the publics' insurance premiums. On my way to the airport today I noticed a billboard that claimed insurance fraud costs every American $1,300 a year. It was likely sponsored by the insurance fraud protection organization or some similar group. It is no wonder jurors believe every case is fraudulent and come into the courtroom believing the plaintiff is a fraud until we, the lawyers, convince them otherwise.

During voir dire, I ask the judge to inquire if any of the potential jury members believe an award in this case will affect anyone other than the two parties, including themselves. The defense attorney always objects to this question because he knows some jurors will naturally say yes. When I am lucky enough to convince the judge to ask it, sure enough, several jurors will claim they believe it will affect their insurance premiums.

Unfortunately, the next question the judge asks is usually, "Even though you feel that way, can you still be fair and impartial?"

The jurors always say, "Yes, I believe I can." I try to question that answer and follow up with a few more questions to asking if they are sure, hoping the judge will excuse them for cause, and I am successful at it from time to time. But if a juror is determined to sit on a jury, it is very difficult to get him to admit that he cannot be fair and impartial. I usually have to use one of my challenges to remove jurors like these.

Second, the defense medical experts, who are trained professional witnesses, can easily claim your client's injuries were preexisting. Without the right ammunition, the plaintiff's trial attorney is in a difficult spot and the insurance carriers know it.

COMMON SOFT-TISSUE INJURIES

Hopefully, the following anatomy lesson will assist you in not only intelligently cross-examining a defense medical expert but also credibly showing the jury how your client was injured. Every plaintiff's personal injury attorney should be familiar with these body parts, as 90 percent of your cases will be comprised of injuries to the neck, back, shoulders, knees, and the temporomandibular joints (TMJ).

In my opening statement, I introduce the jury to the portion of anatomy where my client was injured, first as a whole and then by region. Then, I break it down even further to the individual disc or joint that is injured. I am often accused of testifying as a medical expert when I do this, but I am always sure to say that "the evidence and testimony will show," or "Dr. Vesper will tell you that the spine...."

The Spine

When I introduce the spine to the jury, I start by telling them that it is divided into four parts: the *cervical* or neck region, the *thoracic* or middle back, the *lumbar* or lower back, and the *sacrum* or tailbone. I then draw a *sagittal*, or sideways, version of the head and all four levels of the spine and label them for the jury. This is important to do because by the time your opening statement is through, the jury will know what injuries you are claiming, the anatomy of the human body, and will be at least a little familiar with the relevant anatomy when the doctors begin to testify.

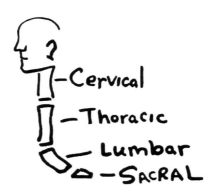

Hand Drawn Example: The Spine

It is absolutely necessary to explain what a disc is, what the levels of the spine are, and what procedures were performed—including what that particular procedure actually is. I recently watched the opening statement of a very good plaintiff's trial attorney and was amazed that he spouted out medical terminology in his opening that he never defined, nor did he explain the anatomy, acting as if the jury was familiar with this stuff. As a person who is familiar with the terminology, even I had trouble following along.

If your client underwent a *microdiscectomy* of the L4-L5 disc of the lumbar spine, I suggest you first tell the jury what the L4-L5 disc is, where it is located, why it has two numbers, and what a microdiscectomy is. The word is misleading and a perfect example of the kind of thing the defense bar will go after. They'll falsely claim, or suggest, that it is a minor procedure because the word *micro* is inserted prior to discectomy. In actuality, it means that the discectomy, which is an open procedure, is performed with the assistance of a microscope. This is just one example and reason you need to know and understand the medicine.

The Cervical Spine

When I discuss the spine, I focus in on the affected region. In a case where my client has received a soft-tissue injury to her neck, I explain that evidence and testimony will show that the cervical spine is made of seven vertebral bodies labeled C, for cervical, and numbered one through seven. I then draw the below image and explain each disc has two numbers, one for the bone above and one for the bone below. For example, the C2-C3 disc is between the C2 and C3 vertebrae. I then draw in the thecal sac, spinal cord, nerve roots, and transverse processes. I further explain that the space between the back edge of a normal disc and the thecal sac is about a millimeter, so the slightest protrusion of the disc outward can cause serious problems and pain.

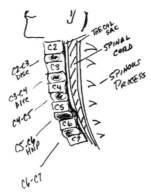

Hand Drawn Example: The Cervical Spine

I also draw an axial view when I present the injured area. I provide the jury with different views to familiarize them with what they will see and hear when the radiologist presents the MRI films during direct examination.

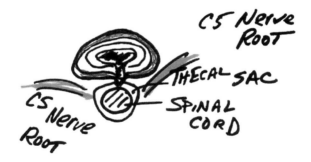

Hand Drawn Example: Axial View

The Discs of the Spine

After discussing the injured area of my client's spine, I further break things down and focus in on an individual spinal disc. I explain what its function is and what *normal, bulging,* and *herniated* discs are. Since I already explained what the spine looks like from the side and have already drawn herniated discs from above and from the side, I then draw the normal, bulging, and herniated discs from above once more to show the differences that they will hear throughout the trial. This gives the jury a foundation for the medicine they will soon be hearing and makes it easier to understand from the get go.

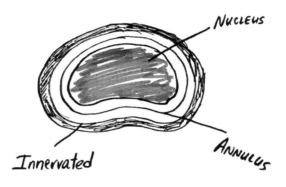

Hand Drawn Example: Normal Disc

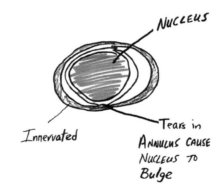

Hand Drawn Example: Bulging Disc

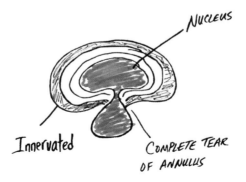

NUCLEUS

Innervated

COMPLETE TEAR
OF ANNULUS

Hand Drawn Example: Herniated Disc

The Knee

With regard to the knee, terms like *medial, posterior horn,* and *anterior lateral horn* can be very confusing for the jury. Like I have said numerous times throughout this book, you *must* understand the medicine well enough to explain it so a layperson, like a juror, can easily understand the terminology and anatomy. More importantly, you must understand it well enough so you can successfully cross-examine a board-certified orthopedic surgeon intelligently and effectively.

The *meniscus* is a shock absorber or padding for the knee joint. It is made of cartilage that is often described as having the consistency of calamari—rubbery and smooth. Because the *distal femur* is shaped like a cartoon bone or dog biscuit and the *proximal tibia* has a plateau, or is flat, they do not connect properly without the meniscus. The following illustrations depict how I present this in court so a juror can easily understand it. The meniscus consists of two menisci: the lateral or outside meniscus, and the medial or inside meniscus.

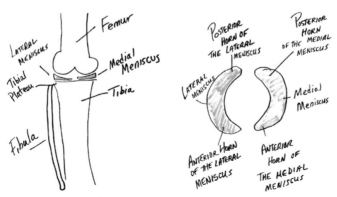

Hand Drawn Examples: The Knee

Torn Meniscus

A torn meniscus could be on the posterior (back) or anterior (front) horn of the lateral (outside) or medial (inside) menisci. Above is a view of the right knee as if you amputated the leg at the knee joint and were looking down into the knee. It can be torn in various ways: a partial tear, which is considered a grade one or grade two tear, or a full thickness tear, which is a complete or grade three tear.

Someone can also suffer a *bucket handle tear*. A bucket handle tear is just like what it sounds like, a u-shaped tear that if you lift it up it looks just like the handle on a bucket. Some ethnicities are predisposed to having what is called a *discoid meniscus* or a meniscus that looks like a Frisbee. This type of meniscus is more prevalent in the Asian community and is also more susceptible to tearing.

The following are the various examples of how I illustrate the types of tears I just discussed, including a complete tear of the anterior horn of the lateral meniscus.

Hand Drawn Example: Types of Tears

False Positive MRI Findings

The knee is notorious for revealing false positive MRI findings. I have had hundreds of knee injury cases with positive MRI findings indicating a torn meniscus where the doctor has discovered during surgery that there is actually no tear at all. In those instances, the doctor then performs a *debridement* or shaving of the macerated edge of the meniscus.

It is still surgery and explains why some doctors say, "let me look in there anyway," despite whether the MRI says there is a finding or not. They perform an arthroscopic surgery and go in with a camera. If they find a tear they repair it; if they do not they just clean it up a bit. I often argue with defense attorneys who claim there was not even a tear when they looked inside. I tell them my client still had to have a surgery on her knee, and if not for their negligent client, she would not have had knee surgery, period.

THE SHOULDER

The shoulder is another body part where common soft-tissue injuries can occur. It is a very complex structure, but by drawing a simple diagram you can show jurors how it functions, what part is injured, and why it will not function the same again. The most common shoulder injuries are torn rotator cuffs and torn labrums. The rotator cuff consists of four muscles. The largest and most commonly injured is the supraspinatus muscle that connects the shoulder to the scapular. The labrum is a piece of cartilage within the shoulder socket. The example below shows how I illustrate the ways these muscles function within the bones, tendons, and ligaments of the upper arm and shoulder area for the jury.

Hand Drawn Example: Shoulder

Torn Rotator Cuff of the Shoulder

The rotator cuff can be completely or partially torn (just like with the knee joint), and MRIs often reveal false positive findings. I cannot tell you how many times an MRI of the shoulder showed a rotator cuff tear and arthroscopic inspection revealed either a *glenoid labral tear* or no tear at all. It is not uncommon for a client to have an impingement syndrome and have to have a piece of the clavicle dissected to allow more room for movement. Although this condition is typically degenerative, you can argue that the accident aggravated a previous asymptomatic condition that then required surgical intervention.

TEMPOROMANDIBULAR JOINTS (TMJs)

The TMJs are the ball and socket joints that attach the jawbone (mandible) to the skull (cranium) in an area called the temporal bone (thus, temporomandibular joint). The jawbone has a ball on the end of it called the mandibular condyle. There is a ball and socket on both sides of your jaw: the left TMJ and the right TMJ. The mandibular condyle fits into a socket in your skull or temporal bone.

At the ball and socket joint, there is a disc, or meniscus, that's not unlike a disc in the spine or the meniscus in the knee. Just like in the cervical spine, when whiplash occurs the ligaments and tendons attached to your jawbone can hyper-extend. If your head is slung forward, it will eventually stop because it is attached to your neck, but your jawbone will continue moving due to inertia, causing the muscles, tendons, and ligaments to stretch, which forces the disc to displace either anteriorly or posteriorly. The disc is then trapped in the forward or backward position and is not recaptured when you open and close your mouth. When this disc displaces, it can cause clicking or popping, can cause your jaw to lock, and can even make it difficult to fully open your mouth. Below are diagrams of the skull and jawbone and a normal and displaced temporomandibular joint.

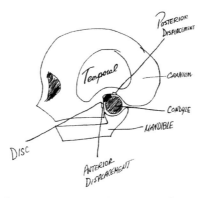

Hand Drawn Example: Normal TM Joint

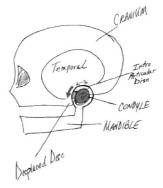

Hand Drawn Example: Displaced TM Joint

PERMANENCE

To prove an injury is permanent, the plaintiff's physician should testify to a reasonable degree of medical probability that the body part is injured and will not function normally again, even with further treatment. As I demonstrated with the spine above, I discuss this at length with the jury by showing four things: the function of the body part, how it functions, what the injury is, and how it affects the body part's ability to function.

Chapter Takeaways

◆ The most common soft-tissue injuries resulting from car accidents are injuries to the neck and back.

◆ Injuries to the knee, shoulder, and jaw can also occur in car accidents.

◆ Drawing the anatomy in your opening statement can give the jury a preview of the injuries you are claiming and help them better understand the anatomy when the doctors begin testifying.

◆ I draw the anatomy in two planes, the same planes the MRIs will later depict so the jurors get a better handle on what they are actually looking at.

◆ When explaining the anatomy of the spine and referring to the spinal discs, explain to the jury that although they will hear two letters and two numbers when describing spinal discs, this only refers to a single disc and its location between the vertebral bodies.

◆ Have your doctors use the term "reasonable degree of medical probability" to prove injuries as this correlates with the preponderance of the evidence standard.

16

THE DIAGNOSIS

Diagnosis is not the end, but the beginning of practice.

Martin H. Fischer

The diagnosis in any medical scenario consists of four things:

1. History

2. Complaints and symptoms

3. Diagnostic test results

4. Physical examination findings

Any physician will tell you that a diagnosis is not created from single piece of information but from the entire puzzle. A doctor cannot rely on a single element, such as a physical examination, to make a proper diagnosis. Despite a favorable history with no prior injuries to the spine, complaints and symptoms that began immediately following the accident, positive EMGs and MRIs, and positive objective and subjective findings from physical exams with treating physicians (including spasm and decreased

ROM) defense doctors often ignore numbers one through three and come to their own diagnosis based on a single ten-minute physical exam. This exam is known as the defense medical examination (DME).

Not to be confused with an independent medical examination (IME), the DME is exactly that, a defense medical examination. These defense exams are a tool the defense uses to highlight any inconsistencies that occur during a patient's long and painful treatment and recovery phase following an accident. Naturally, over the course of seeing numerous doctors, giving histories to numerous doctors and their staff, speaking with insurance companies, being deposed, answering interrogatories, and being examined by numerous defense doctors, a patient's complaints, symptoms, and histories can be utilized to attack their credibility.

You can use the pie chart below in your opening statement, the direct examination of your client's treating physician, and on cross-examination to clarify that a diagnosis involves *all* the factors represented by the slices of pie and not just a single slice, such as a physical exam.

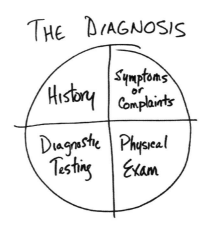

Hand Drawn Example: Diagnosis Pie Chart

Defense doctors love to use their own physical exam findings, recorded usually three to four years following the traumatic event, to opine that the patient had a normal physical exam and thus was not injured. They ignore the history, your client's objective diagnostic test results, the physical exam findings that were positive on dozens of other doctor visits, and the pertinent findings from any other visit—including to the emergency room.

I just completed a trial where my client was a sixty-six-year-old woman who had lived on this earth for 22, 265 pain-free days before an accident caused her severe neck pain. That is exactly how I argued the case. She had severe degeneration and arthritis of her cervical spine, along with three disc bulges. Thankfully, the jury believed her and awarded her a substantial verdict. On its surface, this case was very difficult to prove and that was probably why the insurance company took a chance trying it. That did not work out so well for them.

I used the diagnosis pie chart to clarify that when the history is taken into account—the 22,265 days prior to the accident without a single neck complaint, no prior treatment for her neck, no prior accidents, and no lawsuits—the jury could easily see the defendant's negligence was a substantial factor in bringing about her injuries.

Naturally, I also used the domino theory. For the first time since I have been using the dominos, the defense counsel tried to steal my thunder. In his summation, he told the jury that I was going to use them, and that I was going to line them up to demonstrate that the defendant's negligence had caused all of the things that followed. I thought he did a good job explaining proximate cause for me. And sure enough when I closed, I brought out the dominos. I told the jury that defense counsel stole my thunder, but I was going to show them anyway because they were "so cool." They all laughed. I could see them really enjoying the demonstration.

In fact, this demonstration was different from others I have done, as I had no place to set up the dominos. I typically use the jury rail or even bring in a table or two, but this courtroom prevented me from doing both due to its layout and lack of a jury rail. What I did have was a long counsel table that housed the plaintiff's and defense's attorneys, their clients, and their files.

As I began the demonstration on my side of the table (which was clear of debris) and moved down the table into the defense area, I told defense counsel, without missing a beat, to move his stuff, which he did and the demonstration went the entire length of the table with the last dominos falling right in front of him and his client. It was priceless.

The reason I explain this, is because the way I present a case is very different than many of the lawyers I respect and admire. I never copied anyone's style, although I have borrowed much from many different attorneys. You absolutely must remain true to yourself, keep your own identity, and do what is most comfortable for you.

This case was a perfect example of how to try a soft-tissue case even with the most severe preexisting degeneration and arthritis. You must utilize all of the pieces of the diagnosis puzzle. The history could be the most important piece if you can demonstrate that the plaintiff had lived for so long without any problems. The arthritis and degeneration was obviously there before the accident, but it was not causing her any symptoms. The MRI stated she had bone spurring, a disc ridge complex, and three right-sided bulges. There was also stenosis in her right C4-5 and C5-6 foramina, and the bone spur was contributing to it. The word "contributing" was the key factor. I drew a foramina, which is basically a circle depicting the hole, and placed a bone spur inside it, but the larger blockage of the hole I depicted with the right sided bulge. The MRI report stated that the spur was contributing to it, not the bulge, so the bulge must have been the more significant cause of the stenosis. Then by using the sub-acute positive C6 radiculopathy, which was taken five months after the accident, I proved that the disc bulge occurred within six months since a sub-acute finding is within three to six months. Below is a diagram of the foramina I drew during the trial.

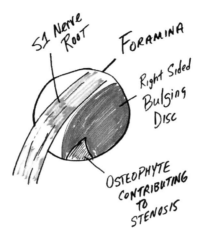

Hand Drawn Example: Foramina

THE DIAGNOSIS AND DEFENSE DOCTORS

The following is an example of what a defense orthopedist will say when on direct examination and then be unable to get out of on cross-examination. With regard to diagnosis, I have heard many a doctor opine that a diagnosis is 90 percent history and 10 percent of the other three pieces of the puzzle. In the case below, the defense doctor testified on direct that a patient's history was 90 percent of the diagnosis. Yet during cross, he couldn't tell me or the jury how he took the plaintiff's history into account.

Defense Orthopedist on Direct

Q: And did you take a history from her?

A: I did.

Q: And I think you talked earlier about a history, with respect to Taylor. But I just wanted to go into this. How important is a history?

A: Well, they teach you back in medical school that you can almost—you can come up with a diagnosis just—in 90 percent of the time—well, 90 percent of the history will give you the diagnosis. The other 10 percent might be the studies or things like that. Back in the day, before you had imaging studies, you know, good doctors used to take a history and be able to diagnose. So, I mean, the history really can be very helpful. So, it is important to take.

Now the Same Defense Orthopedist on Cross

Q: Didn't you just say 90 percent of the diagnosis is the history?

A: Yes.

Q: Right? She never had a prior accident, right?

A: Right.

Q: She complained of pain at the accident scene. Right?

A: Yes.

Q: She went to the emergency room complaining of pain on the VAS scale 8 out of 10. Right?

A: Correct.

Q: She had pain—she had tenderness in her—in her neck, in her trapezius, Right?

A: Correct. That's what she said.

Q: If it's her history—then who cares? How else is it going to be diagnosed in the emergency room? Does it hurt? Yes. Right?

A: Then you like to back it up with some findings.

Q: And—

A: Objective findings—

Q: Other doctors did, thereafter.

A: Okay.

Q: Doctor, did she complain of pain in the emergency room?

A: She did.

Q: Did she complain of pain at the scene of the accident?

A: She did.

Q: Isn't most back pain caused by trauma?

A: Most back pain?

Q: Yeah, isn't it?

A: Sometimes—I mean, a lot are.

Q: Most?

A: Many aren't.

Q: This is a yes or no.

A: It's not yes or no. It really isn't.

Q: Isn't most back pain caused by trauma. Yes or no?

A: No, it's not.

Q: It's not? Okay, great. You have a website, right?

A: Yes.

MR. CAPOZZI: Mark this—as P19, please. Yeah, I'm going to give you one, too.

[Pause in dialog]

MR. CAPOZZI: May I approach?

THE COURT: Yes, counsel.

Q: Doctor, I'm going to show you what's been marked as P19. United Orthopedics. That's your website?

A: That's me.

Q: Read this to the jury. Underlined.

A: "There are many causes of back pain and there's no single explanation for each person. Although, most people experience pain because of an injury or trauma."

Q: Thank you. Isn't that what I just asked you?

A: You said trauma.

Q: She was in a car accident, wasn't she?

A: Sure.

Q: A car accident is trauma, correct?

A: Of course.

As you can see, by researching the defense medical expert's website, in this case an orthopedic surgeon, you can find some real gems for use on cross-examination. If a diagnosis consists of the four parts depicted in the pie chart, then the history cannot be ignored. Defense doctors love to ignore the history or claim it is subjective. Obviously, if the plaintiff or patient is telling her doctor her history, how can it be anything else but subjective? And if the diagnosis is 90 percent history as this doctor opined, then how can the history be ignored? Below is the cross of a defense neurologist regarding his diagnosis of my client.

Defense Neurologist During Cross-Examination

Q: Okay. All right. You talked about a diagnosis, didn't you?

A: Yes.

Q: And in this case you took a history from Ms. Castillo. Correct?

A: Correct.

Q: And the history was that she had no prior history of any injuries or accidents. Correct?

A: Correct.

Q: And then you had all of her medical records. Correct?

A: Whatever they sent me it was.

Q: Yes, whatever you had. And she told you that, basically, on February 13, "I got in an accident." It was a front-end collision. Air bag smacks her in the face. She gets taken by an ambulance to the hospital where she complains of neck pain, ten out of ten. Did you remember that?

A: There was a number given—there's a number that was given there.

Q: Because, it wasn't in your report. Did you know that?

A: [No verbal response.]

Q: You say, "Review of medical records—medical record from St. Joseph's Hospital Medical Center, dated February 13. Describe treatment following motor vehicle accident. Her airbag deployed. No neurological deficits were described in these records. Her head and face were described as atraumatic. X-rays of spine ordered showed no significant degenerative changes. Her symptoms were described as improved upon discharge." You don't think it's important that she was complaining of neck pain ten out of ten at the emergency room?

A: In terms of level, it wasn't critical for the evaluation. She described it as soreness there, also, in the level ten, but it wasn't something that leads to a different opinion.

Q: It wasn't significant to you, correct, in your analysis of her? That's what you're telling this jury?

A: The number ten?

Q: Yes. Isn't that the most pain you could experience? Isn't that what it means? Ten out of ten on a VAS scale?

A: That was her perception of her level of pain, a given ten.

Q: And that's subjective, right, because it's not objective. Right?

A: Well, it certainly is subjective. Yes.

Q: Yes of course. In fact, when she tells you her history that's subjective too, right?

A: It's her recount. It's her recall. It's her perception of what happened.

Q: So, the history is really important, isn't it? It tells you when the onset of these symptoms began and these complaints, right?

A: It's part of the puzzle. It's a piece of the puzzle.

Q: Okay. It's part of the puzzle. So, that's a big part of the puzzle, isn't it? Don't you want to know when the pain started?

A: It's part of it. Yes.

Q: In fact, don't you want to know what she's complaining about?

A: Sure.

Q: Now, when you examined her all you had were the MRI reports, correct?

A: Yes.

Q: And the EMG reports, right? An MRI is an objective test. Is it not?

A: The pictures themselves are not altered by anything. The pictures themselves would be objective pictures. They're changed by—

Q: Isn't it an objective test in a legal sense?

A: I would say, yes, it's an objective test.

Q: Okay. Do you have the two MRI reports of Dr. Amoroso? Do you know Dr. Amoroso?

A: Personally? No.

Q: Do you know his facility, 401 Medical Imaging?

A: Yes.

Q: It's right in Englewood, by you, right?

A: Uh-huh. Yes.

Q: You ever refer patients there?

A: Yes, I do.

Q: Okay. Anyway, you had these MRI reports, correct, when you first examined her?

A: Yes.

Q: You did not have the films, correct?

A: Correct.

Q: Now, can you show me one word in the cervical MRI report that mentions any degenerative finding whatsoever?

A: No.

Q: There's none, right?

A: Correct.

Q: So, in other words, all the information you had—because all you had were the MRI reports, there's not a single word that describes any degenerative findings or anything. Correct?

A: Correct.

Q: But the first thing you write after reviewing only the medical records, MRI reports and taking a history from her is that, a percentage if the population has degenerative disc disease, so she must be within that percentage?

A: Correct.

The plaintiff in the above trial was only twenty years old at the time of the accident. The defense doctor's explanation that she was suffering from degenerative disc disease was completely incredible. Despite the fact that there was no mention on the MRI report of any degenerative findings, coupled with the history, symptoms, complaints, and onset of pain, this doctor still found the plaintiff was not injured—despite all of the pieces of the puzzle of the diagnosis saying otherwise. Not surprisingly, the juries in both of the cases above ultimately found the plaintiffs' injuries were proximately caused by the negligence of both defendants and gave them significant verdicts.

As you know, preponderance of the evidence is the standard of proof in civil cases. In chapter 33 I will explain how to incorporate the diagnosis into your argument to prove proximate cause by a preponderance of the evidence. Although I just explained how to cross-examine a defense doctor regarding the diagnosis, the explanation of a diagnosis in the opening statement should just be the simple drawing and what your client's diagnosis was before you move on to the section of your opening pertaining to the plaintiff's witnesses and experts.

CHAPTER TAKEAWAYS

◆ A diagnosis is a puzzle with four pieces: the history, the complaints and symptoms, the diagnostic testing, and the physical exam findings.

◆ Explain to the jury that you cannot rely on one piece of the puzzle and ignore the other three.

◆ History and onset of symptoms should be 90 percent of the diagnosis.

◆ Break your client's history down into days to enhance the amount of time prior to injury.

◆ Draw a simple pie chart to demonstrate how a doctor comes to a diagnosis by utilizing the four elements.

17

SOLDIERS AND TANKS

A handful of soldiers is always better than a mouthful of arguments.

George C. Lichtenberg

During opening statement, after I explain how a doctor arrives at a diagnosis, I next tell the jury about the people they are going to hear from through live testimony or as mentioned in the medical records or other documents. I list my client's medical providers again, in chronological order from the first treatment to the last, and include their relevant and impressive backgrounds and education. I focus primarily on the medical, liability, and (if necessary) damages experts who I will have testifying on behalf of my client. I consider these witnesses my soldiers and tanks. Not to the jury of course, but to myself. My lay witnesses, including the plaintiff, are my soldiers. My expert witnesses are my army tanks, my big guns, my weapons of mass destruction.

When I choose a jury, I think it is important to learn where the jurors went to college, what they do for a living, and any other unique experiences they may reveal. I listen attentively to these responses so that I can mold the case to fit one or more particular jurors.

I love to indicate where my experts went to medical school because they typically attended an Ivy League or prominent university. In one particular case, a woman mentioned that her adult children were both undergraduate students at Yale. Coincidentally, one of my testifying physicians attended Yale Medical School. I must have brought up the fact that he went to Yale Medical School fifty times during the trial, emphasizing how intelligent one must be just to be accepted there. I often have medical experts with very impressive educations, including Harvard, Penn, Cornell, Brown, Princeton, Duke, and Columbia. I tell the jury they are going to hear from the Ivy League All-Star team of experts.

I have also shaped my opening to the occupations of individual jurors. I once had a juror who was in the tire business. When I explained the vertebral disc, I compared it to an automobile tire analogy I knew he could relate to. I explained that a bulging disc was similar to a tire when you hit a pothole and a bubble appeared on the tire but it did not blow out. A herniated disc was when the tire blew out from a pothole.

I also list the plaintiff, defendant, all of the conditional witnesses and eyewitnesses, and briefly discuss the anticipated testimony as well. I always, if possible, have the plaintiff testify last. I also call the defendant and any defense witnesses in my case. I would rather call them as hostile witnesses and cross them on direct, instead of allowing the defense the opportunity to call them on direct and slant their story in their favor. Doing this allows you to sandwich them between all of your favorable witnesses, makes your case-in-chief longer, and gives the defense less of a case. Their only witnesses should be their experts.

This allows you, as the plaintiff's attorney, to control the majority of the trial and when you rest. By calling every fact witness in the case, you leave the defense with only their own expert witnesses. This is obvious to me now after many years of trial experience. However, you must have extreme confidence to call one or more hostile witnesses in your case-in-chief. So for you new comers, this may be something you want to wade into gradually, instead of diving right into the deep end of the pool.

THE ENEMY SOLDIERS AND TANKS

Just like I discuss the witnesses for the plaintiff and what their anticipated testimony will be with the jury, I also discuss the defense witnesses with them. I literally write out their names, including the defendant and the relevant information that the jury will hear primarily on cross-examination. The defendant has already been deposed, has given a statement to the police and their insurance company, and has answered interrogatories. Their testimony should be anticipated and clearly explained to the jury. With regard to the defense medical experts, I tell the jury what the evidence and testimony will show while I write out their names. I include the number of defense exams they perform per year and whatever bias information I have on a particular defense expert. I also include information from prior court proceedings, as shown in this example from an opening statement I gave last year:

> I know for a fact that Dr. Wurst has performed over 12,000 medical exams in the last twelve years and never found a single soft-tissue injury that was causally related to an accident of any kind—despite the overwhelming evidence you will hear, including from the defense expert himself, that these injuries are often caused by trauma. Their other expert has examined 6,000 persons from the ages of sixteen to ninety and

also has never found a single person's injury caused by trauma. In fact, Dr. Goldberg has testified that every one of those persons, whether sixteen or nineteen, is suffering from a preexisting condition—the same testimony he will give here this week. These doctors appear in court for the defense twenty to thirty times per year, more than any lawyer in the state. Ladies and gentleman, when a doctor appears in court more than a lawyer, their motivation must be explored. Ask yourselves, what is this doctor's motivation? You will learn their motivation is money, and that money affects their credibility when their testimony is against the weight of not only the medical facts in this case but the medical facts relied upon by the entire medical community.

Like I mentioned, I write out the names of the defense doctors and the pertinent information I have gathered throughout my career dealing with these fellows. When I discuss the money they earn, I multiply their annual earnings by the years they have been practicing to achieve much higher amounts that may resonate with a juror and, remarkably, may be incorporated into the verdict the jury later awards. I typically obtain this information on the cross-examination of the defense expert and use it in my closing. However, sometimes I am familiar with the defense doctor and bring it out in my opening. I once received a verdict identical to the amount of money the defense expert made in a single year. It might have been a coincidence, but the amount was identical to the dollar. Additionally, it clarifies just how much these doctors are earning by performing simple so-called medical exams with no doctor-patient relationship, and giving slanted, biased, incorrect, and exaggerated diagnoses and opinions.

CHAPTER TAKEAWAYS

• Expert witnesses are like army tanks, the more you have the easier the battle will be.

• Listen to the jurors' responses regarding their education, experience, and occupation and try to use phrases and analogies they can relate to.

• List all of the witnesses the plaintiff will call in her case-in-chief and generally what they will testify to.

• List all of the defense witnesses, including their doctors. Explain to the jury what you know about these doctors from experience, including their income and obvious bias.

• Call as many fact and expert witnesses as you are comfortable with to lengthen the plaintiff's case-in-chief and shorten the defense's case-in-chief.

18

DAMAGES IN OPENING STATEMENT

A man who dares to waste one hour of life has not discovered the value of life.

Charles Darwin

Unlike most attorneys, I spend little to no time asking for money during my opening statement. The only time I mention noneconomic damages is at the very end of my summation. In cases that insurance companies, and the public due to insurance company propaganda, perceive as lower value cases, such as neck and back soft-tissue cases with little treatment, I may not mention money at all.

The jury knows why you are there. The defense reminds them about a hundred times that the case is about money, money the greedy plaintiff wants them to give to her. So I have nothing else to say regarding money in my opening statement. However, I do lay out all the pain and suffering, the loss of enjoyment of life, the treatment, and any other problems my client has and still endures since the accident. This sets up the dominos in the minds of the jurors. I think the argument for noneconomic damages is better placed in your summation, after you have proven your case, after the evidence is in, and after your client and experts have testified to the noneconomic damages your client has suffered.

There is no exact science to this theory of mine, only that I am personally more comfortable asking for money after all the facts are in. I know attorneys who spend half of their opening discussing damages and that is fine, it's their trial and they can try it any way they like. However, I cannot ask for money for noneconomic damages in my opening, it's not in my make-up, it's not comfortable for me, and so I just do not do it.

In New Jersey, where I try 99 percent of my cases, the plaintiff is precluded from requesting a specific sum for noneconomic damages. We cannot say to the jury, "we are seeking one million dollars and this is why." The amount of noneconomic damages is left solely to the province of the jury. Perhaps that is why I do not discuss it in my opening.

Economic damages are a different story. I always discuss economic damages in my opening. We can explain to the jury the exact amount of economic damages and I always do. For example, if my client lost six weeks of work and was taking home $500 per week, her net loss would be $3,000. All economic losses must be given using the net loss to your client, not the gross loss, so if you do not have an expert, make sure you ask your client her take-home amount of lost income and not gross.

Another typical element of economic damages is the amount of outstanding medical bills the plaintiff incurred as a result of the accident. The amount of outstanding medical bills should be discussed in opening statement, listed, and added up. The amount should be usual and customary and the treatment necessary and causally related to the injuries your client suffered as a result of the defendant's negligence.

At the Conclusion of the Evidence

The last section of my opening statement is a brief sentence or two:

> After all the evidence is in, and you hear from all the witnesses and see all of the documented evidence in the case, I will come back to speak to you and explain how Ms. Jones proved all the elements needed to prevail in this matter. Thank you.

While I am saying this I refer to the chart I drew in the beginning of my opening with the four elements needed to prove the case. This is the exact outline I use in every trial. Memorizing this outline allows me to open in any case by just knowing the facts.

Chapter Takeaways

- Personally, I do not use the term "money" in my opening.

- With regard to noneconomic damages, depending on what you are permitted to argue, explain the losses and harms suffered by your client. Depending on your comfort level, discuss that your client is here to be compensated with money.

- Always detail economic damages in your opening statement, including the exact amounts of net lost income and the exact amounts of any outstanding medical bills that are causally related to the defendant's negligence.

19

PROVING THE PLAINTIFF'S CASE

War is hell.

General William Tecumseh Sherman

Proving the plaintiff's case at trial is what it is all about. The domino theory chronologically details all the facts of the case, including the diagnosis of the plaintiff's injuries, and allows the jury to connect the defendant's negligence with the accident and resultant injuries. If you lay out your dominos as if you were preparing your summation, it will assist you in discovering exactly what testimony you need to elicit from witnesses at trial to prove your case. In other words, if you are going to use the dominos, you better use the medical reports, diagnostic test reports, and diagnostic films or data to explain every one of them.

Keep Your Exhibits Easy to Understand

You must have creative, easy to understand—I repeat—easy to understand exhibits. I have tried several different ways to demonstrate injuries or liability. One exhibit I have tweaked and tweaked is the timeline, as domino theory is based on it.

You must be clear and concise. If you are going to list every single doctor's appointment your client attended, then they should be color coordinated by doctor or type of treatment. Surgeries should stand out from a follow-up, procedures should stand out from physical therapy, and so on. I think if you list the key treatments and fill in the blanks orally, or "rhetorically flourish" as Rodney Jew would say, the timeline is much clearer and easier to understand. You should also call the treating physician—or all of them if you can pull it off financially.

Use the Dominos to Set up Damages

The damages all flow from and include what is described on the individual dominos. This can include the airbag deploying like a shotgun blast to the face, the treatment that takes course over months, driving to and from the doctor's office, waiting to be seen and then undergoing painful physical therapy or even being placed under general anesthesia to have a surgical procedure or injections, the painful diagnostic tests including the EMG, and obviously the effect of the accident and injuries on a person's ability to carry out their daily activities. When I try a case, I set out to have every treating doctor testify in court. I have called as many as eleven physicians at trial.

MAKE THE CASE BIG

Another reason I call every doctor who has treated the plaintiff is because the trial lasts longer. The plaintiff's case takes at least a week to complete. I often try to spill it over to the second week, so the testimony is still fresh during the week the verdict will be delivered. I also call the defendant in my case-in-chief and as many witnesses the defense may be calling to take the wind out of their sails and reduce the number of witnesses they get to actually call in their case. I want the trial to last longer so it appears to the jury that this case is big. Not only does the jury sense the case is valuable due to the amount of time the trial lasts and the amount of witnesses that are produced, it also helps set up a settlement at trial.

The adjuster is usually present and they will sit there for days as you put on your case. The longer the adjuster is present, it allows him more time to consider settling the matter. Also, I do not know any lawyer who wants to cross-examine five to ten plaintiff's experts in a single trial. Remember, I consider my experts like army tanks. If I have ten and the defense has two, who do you think is going to win the battle?

I often call the plaintiff last. I also have as many of the plaintiff's friends, family members, and colleagues testify before I call the plaintiff to the stand. This allows the jury to hear all of the issues the plaintiff is experiencing from others before hearing it right out of the horse's mouth. Most importantly, it allows the plaintiff to hear the case and to understand what I am trying to do and anticipate what testimony I will try to elicit from him.

Chapter Takeaways

- Chronologically lay out the history of the plaintiff before and after the negligence of the defendant to set up the dominos in the minds of the jurors.

- Use easy to understand exhibits.

- Call as many fact witnesses as you need.

- Call all of your experts.

- If possible, call the plaintiff last so they can get into the flow of the trial before being put on the stand.

20

DIRECT EXAMINATION OF THE PLAINTIFF

The most important kind of freedom is to be what you really are. You trade in your reality for a role. You trade in your sense for an act. You give up your ability to feel, and in exchange, put on a mask. There can't be any large-scale revolution until there's a personal revolution on an individual level. It has to happen inside first.

Jim Morrison

Great plaintiffs don't need coaching. I often underprepare my clients for trial because I do not want them to sound robotic, rehearsed, or use words that they don't typically use in everyday life. In other words, you don't want your client to sound like a lawyer. I simply walk my clients through the topics we will discuss and tell them to tell the truth, not exaggerate, and speak from their hearts. When people tell the truth and speak from their hearts, the testimony they give is authentic and radiates honesty. The jury will be able to relate to what your clients have experienced and are still dealing with on a daily basis.

I begin my direct examination of the plaintiff with her date of birth and age. I do this because I have used the timeline in my opening, and I want to lay the foundation for the dominos from the beginning of her life. I chronologically walk her though her life before the accident. We then discuss the accident and her treatment after the accident. I also try to reiterate that all her pain and suffering stemmed from the accident itself.

I emphasize that leading up to the one second before the defendant's negligence caused the accident, there were absolutely no symptoms, no treatments, and no other lawsuits. I would imagine this is the standard direct for most lawyers, and my direct is nothing more than discussing each of the plaintiff's case facts in chronological order. I am doing nothing other than setting up the dominos in the jurors' minds.

I used to write out my direct examinations and read the questions to the witness. But, just like in a deposition, when you write out questions you sometimes do not listen to the answer and just ask your next question. By doing that you fail to properly follow-up. Although you may know the pertinent issues, you take for granted that the jurors understand the issues as well as you and you fail to elaborate on them.

Ultimately, the jurors do not get to hear the subtle elaborations on your client's answers because you failed to follow them up correctly. I also feel that reading questions off a sheet of paper makes your client's testimony sound robotic and unnatural. I now ask questions without any notes at all. Knowing your case inside out allows you to deal with any complications that arise because you really know the case and you know your cause is the correct one.

I realize this is not an easy task. It takes years of trial experience to memorize the order of effective questions for a plaintiff. You must talk about the person, the accident, the treatment, and especially the damages. I did not always put on my cases without written questions for direct examination. In fact, when I began, I wrote down not only the questions, but also how to lay the foundation, mark evidence for identification, and even the notes on how to offer items into evidence.

LAY THE PROPER FOUNDATION

Because I knew the rules and procedures to offer documents into evidence (I copied it verbatim onto my direct exam cheat sheet), I learned how much judges really appreciate it when procedure is followed correctly. It is hard to fathom how many lawyers, and lawyers who have tried dozens of cases, cannot even lay a foundation or offer a document into evidence properly. The most common error I see is when a lawyer tries to impeach a witness with a deposition transcript. Below is an example of how to mark something for identification, lay the foundation, and offer it into evidence. These exhibits were photographs of the property damage to my client's car following a chain reaction collision.

Q: May I approach Your Honor? Can I have these marked? I am going to show you what has been marked P-1 through P-4 for identification, do you recognize these?

A: Yes.

Q: What are they?

A: Photographs.

Q: What is depicted in the photographs?

A: Cars that were in an accident.

Q: Do you recognize this vehicle?

A: That's my Pathfinder.

Q: What color was your Pathfinder?

A: White.

Q: What type of car were you driving on the night of the accident?

A: My white Pathfinder.

Q: Did you see your car following the accident?

A: Yeah, at the junkyard when I went to get my personal belongings.

Q: Prior to the accident, did your car have any property damage to it whatsoever?

A: No, it was in perfect condition.

Q: Does P-1 accurately depict the damage to your vehicle as a result of this accident?

A: Yes.

Q: What does this photograph show?

A: The front bumper and grill are all smashed in where I hit the car in front of me.

Q: Lets go though them one by one.

A: Okay.

Q: Does P-2 accurately depict the damage to your vehicle as a result of this accident?

A: Yes.

Q: What does P-2 show?

A: It's the interior of the car. The airbag that deployed and struck me in the face. But it's deflated in the photo.

Q: Does P-3 accurately depict the damage to your vehicle as a result of this accident?

A: Yes.

Q: What does P-3 show?

A: The rear where the car struck me from behind. The trunk is all smashed in and the lights are broken.

Q: Does P-4 accurately depict the damage to your vehicle as a result of this accident?

A: Yes.

Q: What does P-4 show?

A: That's another photo of the car from the side that shows the damage to the front and the back.

Mr. Capozzi: Your Honor, at this time I offer P1 through P4 into evidence. May I publish them to the jury?

I put this example in for new attorneys, less experienced attorneys, or experienced attorneys who just have never done it properly. There is nothing wrong with using notes, cheat sheets, or outlines. However, if you can be effective without them (and you can) do yourself a favor learn to not use them. You will appear much more organized and more prepared without the burdensome tablets, pads, or piles of paper that otherwise sit on an already crowded counsel table in a courtroom.

Properly laying the foundation for documents, marking them for identification, offering them into evidence, and either publishing them to the jury or just using them to question a witness is necessary for all witnesses you call in your case or cross-examine, not just the plaintiff. When you put your medical experts on the stand or cross the defense medical experts, you need to lay the foundation for every medical record, film, or treatise. The smoother you execute this task, the smoother your case will go.

In any injury case, it is important to understand your client's pain and history. We do not go to the doctor's office without feeling some sort of pain or discomfort. Your client's subjective complaints are the basis for their treatment. The defense often argues that the pain the plaintiff experienced is exaggerated or subjective. Do not fall into the trap of what is objective or subjective, you need both and the two go hand in hand. It starts with your client's subjective pain that leads to the objective tests that corroborate her pain. The accident is the cause of your client's pain. The domino theory will make this a simple task for the jury to decide. Without the defendant's initial negligence, the accident, pain, and objective medical tests and diagnosed injuries would not have occurred.

CHAPTER TAKEAWAYS

◆ Do not over prepare your witnesses. This includes not allowing them to use legalese that will show they've been over prepared.

◆ Listen to the your witness's answers so your next question does not leave out important information.

◆ Tell your client to tell their story from their heart.

◆ Know your case so well that you do not need notes of any kind.

◆ Properly lay the foundation of photographs and documents so your case appears organized and it appears you know what you are doing.

◆ Your client's pain alone cannot hold the day, but must be fleshed out to corroborate the objective medical testing that occurs later to prove your client's injury.

21

Direct Examination of the Plaintiff's Physicians

I fear not the man who has practiced 10,000 kicks once, but I fear the man who has practiced one kick 10,000 times.

Bruce Lee

When people are injured in falls or automobile accidents they usually suffer musculoskeletal injuries. These injuries include fractures, herniated spinal discs, and tears in their muscles, ligaments, or tendons. In these cases, the first physician they should consult with is an orthopedist. If they are taken to the emergency room via ambulance and have a comminuted or displaced fracture, they will usually undergo an open surgery that will require hardware. If the fracture is nondisplaced, they are usually casted and sent home. Obviously every injury is different and therefore the treatment is different.

With regard to soft-tissue injuries, these are typically not dealt with in the ER. The patients are x-rayed, determined to be fracture free, and are discharged with instructions to follow up with their primary care physicians. Many people do just that after they are home and the pain either continues or worsens. Their primary care physicians usually medicate and refer them to physical therapy or an orthopedist. Many others go see a lawyer or a chiropractor.

Defense lawyers love when a plaintiff does not seek treatment with their primary care physician and either seeks treatment with a chiropractor or, even better, sees a lawyer. The timeline of medical treatment immediately following an accident is instrumental in proving causation, and the defense typically attacks the credibility of a plaintiff, their physicians, and even their attorney regarding this sequence of events. There are many reasons a plaintiff consults with an attorney immediately following an accident, and there is nothing wrong with it.

The most common reason I encounter is that the person has never been involved in an accident and does not understand how their medical bills are going to be paid. As many doctors do not accept auto insurance or treat people involved in auto accidents, the client ends up going on a wild goose chase to find a doctor who accepts automobile personal injury protection insurance (PIP). This is a very common and important issue for plaintiffs and their attorneys because the last thing you want to deal with are outstanding medical bills that were payable by the plaintiff's automobile insurance carrier and were not paid because an unknowing physician attempted to bill their private insurance carrier and the bills were denied. If the attorney or client is not on top of this situation, the bills go unpaid and the possibility of settling the case goes down the drain because the outstanding bills are not boardable and thus need to be incorporated into the settlement. Unfortunately, this is very common. In order to alleviate this issue, many attorneys have a network of doctors they deal with regularly in order to assure the patient gets quality treatment and their bills get paid in a timely fashion.

However, defense attorneys attempt to use this information to discredit the plaintiff and, in doing so, cast a shadow of doubt on the whole accident and injury. This is the fraud defense: the client, lawyer, and doctors are all conspiring to commit fraud and collect money for a nonexistent injury or preexisting condition. This scenario falls right in step with the insurance companies' fraud propaganda campaign and, if not dealt with properly, can derail even the most meritorious injury claim.

There are several ways to deal with the lawyer referral scenario. The first line of defense is the attorney-client privilege. Naturally, any conversation between a lawyer and a client is confidential. If you have referred your client to a doctor, for whatever reason, this conversation is privileged and any inquiry into what was discussed must be objected to during the deposition. This will alert the defense attorney that you referred your client, but who cares? You can always keep this issue out of trial as its prejudice is significantly outweighed by the relevance. Not only is it prejudicial to the client, but it's worse for you as the attorney as you will also be looked at cock-eyed by the jury.

You will never be able to right that wrong in a courtroom. Thus, this must be kept out at trial. The best way to handle this issue is by giving the client a list of all physicians in the area that accept PIP insurance, and let the client choose who they wish to treat with. This is similar to the list of providers that a health insurance company gives to their insured.

The direct examination of your client's physicians is your opportunity to prove how qualified your experts are in the particular areas of medicine that involve your client and are the key medical issues in the case. I rarely use chiropractors in a soft-tissue case, only calling them in addition to the orthopedist, radiologist, neurologist, or pain management doctors—and only when I know them and know they will only help me and not hurt me. There are many people who believe chiropractors are like witch doctors and not qualified to give opinions. This is especially true in the face of a defense orthopedist who opines that chiropractic medicine is harmful to treating a herniated disc and insinuates that the chiropractic treatment, and not the accident, was the cause of the herniated disc or worsening of the plaintiff's condition following the accident, not the accident itself.

Personally, I have had only good experiences treating with chiropractors, but I am not the jury. We even have a standard juror voir dire question in New Jersey that concerns chiropractors and whether any juror has an opinion regarding chiropractors. I think this question alone sends off red flags regarding the validity of your case, so I choose not to bring in chiropractic experts for the most part, in order to avoid any of that nonsense. The use of an orthopedist gives immediate credibility to your case and the seriousness of the injuries. Do not get me wrong, I have had great results with chiropractic experts, but in my experience medical doctors trump chiropractors, and the defense certainly is not calling a chiropractor.

The direct examination of the plaintiff's physician begins with qualifying your client's physician as an expert in one or more areas of medicine. I typically call a separate expert for each area of medicine needed to prove my case. I believe this is extremely important because the defense often calls one medical expert to testify to several areas of medicine in which they have minimal to no experience.

A perfect example of this is when the defense hires a retired general orthopedic surgeon to opine about a spinal injury. The defense expert will not only have to testify regarding a surgery he has never performed but also to the radiology films, which were not even in existence when he graduated medical school, and to the neurological medicine involved. If the MRI film findings are the objective medical evidence you need to prove a spinal injury case, it is imperative you call the reading radiologist to testify about his findings. The reading radiologist, the surgeon who performed the spine surgery, and the neurologist who performed the EMG are the three key expert witnesses that you must call to prove your case.

On its face, the case is about injured discs, the surgery, and the nerve involvement stemming from the injured discs. Who better to testify than the three physicians with subspecialties in these exact areas? Right off the bat, you have an advantage because the qualifications of these three individual experts trump the general qualifications of a single defense orthopedist.

SAMPLE QUESTIONS FOR AN ORTHOPEDIST

Here is a sample of direct examination questions for an orthopedist in a soft-tissue case, beginning with the expert's qualifications:

Q: Doctor, can you give the jury the benefit of your education?

Q: And in fact you completed medical school, correct?

Q: Did you at some point obtain a license to practice medicine?

Q: How is that obtained?

Q: After obtaining your license to practice medicine, did you become board-certified?

Q: What is board certification?

Q: And you passed?

Q: Do you have a private practice?

Q: What is the name and where is it located?

Q: What is orthopedics?

Q: Can you prescribe medication?

Q: Do you treat patients with neck and back injuries?

Q: Do you treat patients who have been involved in trauma?

Q: Car accidents?

Q: Fall downs?

Q: Sports injuries?

Q: How many patients have you treated with neck and back injuries in your career?

Q: Do you perform surgery?

Q: What types of surgery do you perform?

Q: Do you perform surgery on the neck and back?

Q: What percentage of the surgeries that you perform are on the neck and back?

Q: How many total surgeries do you perform per year?

Q: How many surgeries have you performed in your career?

Q: As part of your practice, do you regularly rely on the reports of other specialists such as radiologists?

Q: Do you rely on the report of the radiologist or do you read the films as well?

Q: How many films do you read a day/week/month?

Q: Are you trained and educated in interpreting MRI films of the neck and back?

Q: Can you explain the difference between an MRI and an x-ray?

Q: When did MRIs become an accepted modality of radiology?

Q: Was MR imaging part of your medical school education and training?

Q: At this time, I would like to offer Dr. Owens as an expert in the field of orthopedic surgery.

QUESTIONS FOR AN ORTHOPEDIC SURGEON

Q: Doctor, are all of your opinions that you will give today to a reasonable degree of medical probability?

Q: Doctor, what is a diagnosis? History, complaints, diagnostic testing, and physical exam?

Q: Is the history important?

Q: Why?

Q: Can most injuries be linked to a single traumatic event?

Q: What is a spinal disc?

Q: Are there nerves in the disc?

Q: Can you draw the spine, neck, and back for the jury and explain the anatomy?

Q: What is a disc bulge?

Q: What is a disc herniation?

Q: Can trauma such as a car accident cause a disc to bulge?

Q: Herniate?

Q: Can you explain "objective" vs. "subjective"?

Q: At some point, did you to treat Ms. Jones?

Q: When?

Q: What records or documents did you have when she came to see you?

Q: Did you take a history from her?

Q: What was the history she gave you?

Q: What were her complaints?

Q: Did you perform a physical examination of her?

Q: Were there any objective findings on your exam?

Q: What were they?

Q: A patient cannot fake a spasm, correct?

Q: Anything else?

Q: What is a diminished reflex?

Q: At some point did you refer Ms. Jones for MRIs?

Q: Where?

Q: And at some point did you receive the MRI reports from that facility?

Q: You read the films?

Q: I am going to show you what's been marked as P-6. Do you recognize this?

Q: What is it?

Q: MRI Reports?

Q: One lumbar and one cervical?

Q: And I am going to show you what has been marked for identification as P7?

Q: What are these?

Q: Can you show the jury the injuries you discussed on the actual MRI?

Q: What is degeneration?

Q: Was the degeneration caused by this accident?

Q: What is the significance of degeneration?

"The significance of degeneration" is very important. Your entire case will hinge on this issue at trial. The defense, as usual, will claim that your client's injuries were preexisting, or the result of degeneration, and not caused by the accident. You need to make sure your doctor discusses what conditions on the films were preexisting and what were not. In other words, there are old findings and new findings. The doctor must testify that obviously the ridging of bone beneath the disc herniation, which took years to form, was not caused by the accident. However, the disc herniation probably was caused by the accident because disc herniations are painful and the history of no pain prior to the accident and the onset of symptoms immediately following the accident rule out a preexisting disc herniation at that level. Moreover, degeneration makes a person more susceptible to injury.

Additionally, the positive EMG (which was classified as acute and performed within three months of the accident) at the same level as the disc bulge and herniation further proves the disc herniation was caused by the accident. This is a key element in proving your case using the domino theory because the EMG actually dates the bulge or herniation. A finding on an MRI cannot be dated without clinical correlation. This is why the history and onset of symptoms is crucial in formulating a diagnosis.

Q: Doctor did you recommend treatment for Ms. Jones?

Q: Did you refer her for pain management?

Q: Did she receive epidurals?

Q: Did that help her?

Q: Did you recommend surgery?

Q: What type of surgery did you recommend?

Q: Did she receive that surgery?

Q: When?

Q: I'm going to show you what's been marked for identification as P-8. Do you recognize this document?

Q: What is it?

Q: Is this the operative report from her January 18, 2014 surgery?

Q: Does it detail the surgery you performed on Ms. Jones?

Q: At this time I offer P-8 into evidence, Your Honor.

[At this point, I utilize a surgical storyboard that depicts the different steps involved in the surgery. I purchase these from a medical illustration company or evidence store.]

Q: Doctor, I am going to show you what's been marked as P-9 for identification. Does this storyboard accurately depict the surgery you performed on Ms. Jones as described in your operative report?

Q: Will you please walk the jury through the steps you took during the surgery?

Q: Doctor, do you have an opinion, within a reasonable degree of medical probability, whether the disc bulge at C5-6 and the disc herniation at L5-S1 were caused by the accident?

Q: What is that opinion?

Q: Doctor, do you have an opinion within a reasonable degree of medical probability whether the disc bulge at C5-6 and the disc herniation at L5-S1 are permanent?

Q: Why?

Q: Will future treatment cause the organ (the disc) to function normally again even with further medical treatment?

Q: Did you refer Ms. Jones to any other doctors?

Q: Did Dr. Maggiano treat her?

Q: Recommend epidurals?

Q: Did she receive physical therapy?

Q: For how long?

Q: When was the last time you saw Ms. Jones?

Q: To a reasonable degree of medical probability, despite not seeing her for a year, would your opinion change as to her probable prognosis?

Q: Why?

Q: Does a disc have to touch a nerve to be bulging or herniated?

Q: What is discogenic pain?

Q: Hypothetically, if I were to tell you an orthopedist who examined Ms. Jones once for ten minutes opined that her injuries were not caused by this accident but were degenerative, would you agree?

Q: Why not?

As you can see in the above example, an orthopedist is an excellent witness to discuss the anatomy and cause of a soft-tissue injury. The orthopedist who actually performs the surgery must be called to testify at trial, regardless of the cost. When put side by side with a defense orthopedist who saw your client one time for ten minutes and who disagrees with everything the client's treating physicians have opined, the defense has no credibility.

That is why you must also call the reading radiologist to show the jury the actual injuries on the MRI. The radiologist has the most training and experience in this medical subspecialty and your case depends on the jury believing the injuries are present in the first place. Defense experts have a habit of disagreeing with the reading radiologist, often stating that the herniation is a bulge or not even present.

Below is an example from a partial direct examination of a reading radiologist. I do not discuss his qualifications, which should be handled like in the previous example with the orthopedist. But I do give you a few nuggets on the difference between an opinion from a treating physician and an opinion from a radiologist who is not opining on causation but on what the actual findings on the MRI are.

Questions for a Reading Radiologist

Q: Doctor, when you were asked to read these films, did you know there was a lawsuit?

Q: Did you have a history of the patient?

Q: What did the prescription say?

Q: Do you get paid the same amount of money whether you find an abnormality or not on an MRI film?

Q: Did you ever meet Ms. Jones?

[The radiologist can be the most credible expert you call because he has limited information on the patient when he reads the prescription. The history usually states "Neck pain, MVA," or just "neck and back pain." The doctor has no motive to find injury.]

Q: Doctor, you stated all of your opinions would be to a reasonable degree of medical probability, correct?

Q: Do radiologists in their day-to-day practice give opinions on the cause of a finding on an MRI?

Q: You read a film and detail what you see on that film, correct?

Q: So, when I ask you, and you show this jury what is on Ms. Jones's film, are you testifying that there is probably disc herniation at L5-S1?

Q: You have read 100,000 MRI films of the spine, correct?

Q: Do you know the difference between a bulge and a herniation?

Q: Is there a disc herniation at L5-S1?

Q: Are you sure?

Q: You are testifying to 100 percent certainty that there is a disc herniation on that film?

A radiologist who testifies that a disc herniation is present on an MRI does not testify to a medical probability. He testifies it is 100 percent a disc herniation. He sees films everyday, and he clearly knows the difference between a bulge and herniation. This is why you must call the reading radiologist. These examples clearly demonstrate the necessity of calling your client's physicians in order to combat the defense's credibility.

Chapter Takeaways

- Call all of the key physicians to testify at trial to prove the elements you need to prove your case.

- Call doctors with subspecialties that the defense experts do not have.

- Have your doctors explain how important the onset of symptoms is to prove causation.

- Use storyboards to depict the actual surgeries or procedures your client endured.

- Call the radiologist and have him testify to 100 percent certainty.

22

Objective Medical Evidence

A wise man portions his beliefs to the evidence.

David Hume

A limitation on lawsuit or verbal threshold case in New Jersey must be proven through objective credible evidence. The defense is going to hammer this issue *ad nauseam* at trial. Their defense experts will testify that there was no objective evidence of permanent injury during their ten-minute exam. They will say this despite there being a positive objective MRI, despite there being a positive objective EMG, despite there being a positive objective spasm, despite there being a positive objective discogram, and despite there being a positive post-discogram MRI or CT scan.

Use the Treatment Timeline
to Show Objective Evidence

However, this can be easily combatted using the treatment timeline first discussed in chapter 12. Ask your experts whether the following findings on physical exams or performed tests were objective. Walk your experts through each finding and circle each of the objective ones in red. Then do the same with the defense doctors. They will no doubt agree with you that all the items circled in red are objective, not subjective or based on the patient's complaints. The following is a timeline example with the objective findings circled.

Treatment Timeline

April 27, 2007 — Motor vehicle collision

April 27, 2007 — Emergency room: Memorial Hospital (X-ray showing reversal of the cervical spine's normal lordotic curve.)

April 29, 2007 — Dr. Berger, PCP (spasm)

May 1, 2007 — Dr. Lee, chiropractor: three times a week for twelve weeks (spasm)

July 1, 2007 — (MRI of the cervical spine: C5-C6 HNP, MRI of the lumbar spine: L4-5 Bulge, L5-S1 HNP)

July 5, 2007 — Dr. Maggiano, neurologist: initial evaluation (spasm)

July 10, 2007 — (EMG with Dr. Maggiano: C5 Radiculopathy, L5 Radiculopathy)

July 27, 2007 — Dr. Vesper, orthopedist: initial consult (spasm)

July 30, 2007 — Physical therapy three times a week for four weeks

August 4, 2007 — Last chiropractic visit (fifty-seven visits total with(spasm))

September 1, 2007 — Dr. James: initial consultation for pain management((spasm and diminished reflex))

September 14, 2007 — Cervical epidural((fluoroscopy))

September 30, 2007 — Cervical epidural((fluoroscopy))

October 20, 2007 — Cervical epidural((fluoroscopy))

January 12, 2008 — Lumber epidural((fluoroscopy))

January 30, 2008 — Lumber epidural((fluoroscopy))

February 19, 2008 — Lumber epidural((fluoroscopy))

April 14, 2008 — Discogram of the lumbar spine: positive at L4-L5((fluoroscopy images show HNP with annular tear))

April 14, 2008 —(Post-discogram CT scan of the lumbar spine: bulge with annular tear at L4-L5, L5-S1 HNP)

May 1, 2008 — Medial branch block at L4-L5 ((fluoroscopy))

May 30, 2008 — Intradiscal electrothermal annuloplasty (IDET): L4-L5 lumbar spine((fluoroscopy))

June 15, 2008 —(Discogram of the cervical spine: positive at C5-C6 (fluoroscopy))

June 15, 2008 —(Post-discogram CT scan of the cervical spine: C5-C6 HNP)

July 17, 2008 — Orthopedic visit: physical therapy three times a week for eight weeks((spasm))

December 12, 2008 — Last PT visit((diminished ROM and spasm))

January 28, 2009 — Defense exam with Dr. Blood, neurologist: no spasm or objective evidence of permanent injury

January 31, 2009 — Follow up visit with Dr. Maggiano, neurologist: (severe spasm)

February 14, 2009 — Defense exam with Dr. Wurst, orthopedist: no spasm or objective evidence of permanent injury

February 22, 2009 — Follow up with Dr. James, orthopedist: (spasm, limited ROM cervical and lumbar spine)

March 1, 2010 — Today

After going through this exercise with all the medical experts, it will be clear that there is ample objective evidence to prove your case. It will also be clear that the defense expert is clearly relying on his physical exam *only*, and not on the entire puzzle as all the doctors will testify they are required to use to formulate a diagnosis. Explain to the jury how the *only* doctors not to find objective evidence were the defense doctors.

Make it About the Expert's Credibility

In fact, immediately following the defense examinations, send the plaintiff back to his treating doctors so they can once again find objective findings of injury. This is very important. After you receive notice of a defense exam, schedule a plaintiff's exam or have their treating doctors, in the same specialty as the defense doctors, reexamine the plaintiff the same day or as soon thereafter as possible.

It is not easy for a defense doctor to explain how there was a spasm, or some other objective sign of injury, right before and after his exam. It is then the defense doctor's credibility that comes into play and not the plaintiff's. Remember, objective findings are not based on the plaintiff's complaints, thus the credibility of these findings is not in question. Here is a sample cross-examination of a defense neurologist when asked to explain how he is the only doctor to not find any objective evidence.

Q: Doctor, you examined Mrs. Jones on January 28, 2009, correct?

A: Yes, that is correct.

Q: And this was almost two years after the accident?

A: Yes.

Q: And you examined her only one time?

A: Yes.

Q: For ten minutes?

A: Yes, but the exam was longer than that, including the history.

Q: Doctor, you actually had your hands on her, examining her for ten minutes?

A: Yes.

Q: And there was no patient/physician relationship?

A: No there was not, this was an independent medical exam.

Q: Independent? Did the judge ask you to examine her?

A: No.

Q: The defense asked you to examine her, correct?

A: Yes.

Q: So this was a defense exam, not an independent exam?

A: The defense hired me to examine the plaintiff, but the exam is called an independent medical exam or IME.

Q: It should be called a defense medical exam or DME, no?

A: That's not for me to decide.

Q: Doctor, lets go back to your report. In your report dated February 7, 2009, you stated that there were no objective findings of permanent injury correct?

A: Yes, although she did complain of some tenderness on straight-leg raising and lateral bending this was a subjective complaint, not objective.

Q: Spasm is objective correct?

A: Yes.

Q: You can actually feel it with your hands, correct?

A: Yes, that is true, but she did not have any spasm on my exam.

Q: Doctor, you had all of Mrs. Jones's treating records at the time of your exam, correct?

A: Yes.

Q: Isn't it true every doctor that examined her found a spasm on every single examination?

A: I believe so.

Q: In fact, after you examined her, Dr. Maggiano, her treating neurologist, reexamined her three days later and he found a spasm.

A: Let me check, that is correct.

Q: You are the only physician who examined her that did not find a spasm?

A: Dr. Wurst did not find spasm either.

Q: Dr. Wurst?

A: Yes.

Q: The other defense doctor?

A: Yes.

Q: How much did you get paid to perform this exam?

As you can see, it is possible to prove bias against a defense doctor when his findings are adverse to every treating doctor's findings, and he was paid to do so. To further prove there is a ton of objective medical evidence in your case, walk the doctor through all of the treatment and all of the treating doctors' objective findings, including the objective diagnostic test results. When I do this, I circle all of the objective findings in red. When compared to the defense doctor's opinion that there was no objective evidence of injury, it is overwhelming.

Q: Doctor, you told us a spasm is an objective finding correct?

A: Yes.

Q: And the plaintiff cannot fake a spasm?

A: Yes.

Q: On Dr. Lee's first examination after the accident, he found a spasm correct?

A: Yes.

[Circle spasm in red]

Q: He ordered an MRI of the cervical spine, correct?

A: Yes.

Q: An MRI is an objective test, correct?

A: Yes it is.

[Circle MRI cervical in red]

Q: He ordered an MRI of the lumbar spine, correct?

A: Yes.

Q: And we know that's objective too, right?

A: Yes.

[Circle MRI lumbar in red]

Q: She went to see Dr. Maggiano, correct?

A: Yes.

Q: And he found a spasm?

A: Yes.

[Circle spasm in red]

Q: Dr. Maggiano ordered an EMG?

A: Yes.

Q: And we know that's objective too, right?

A: Yes.

[Circle EMG in red]

Continue to walk the doctor through every physician's treat-ment of the plaintiff, including his own exam. It will clearly show there is plenty of objective evidence of injury—with the findings of the defense physicians' examinations as the only ex-ception. By the end of the cross-examination, except for the two defense exams, the entire treatment chart will be circled in red. You can actually show the jury all of the objective evidence of injury and it will be overwhelmingly obvious that the only two doctors who found no objective evidence were the two hired guns the defense offered.

CHAPTER TAKEAWAYS

- Walk the jury through all of the plaintiff's treatment and include the objective physical examination findings as well as objective medical test results.

- Show that the defense medical experts were the only doctors who did not find any objective evidence of injury.

- Send your client to a follow-up examination with their treating doctor the same day (or a day after) as the DME.

- Cross-examine the defense expert on the objective findings and the testing the plaintiff underwent for years before his DME.

- To prove bias, try to show the jury that the DME was ten minutes on one day, years after the accident; there was no patient/physician relationship; and that defense physicians get paid.

23

PREPARING TO CROSS-EXAMINE THE DEFENSE MEDICAL EXPERT

That reliability be assessed in a particular manner: by testing in the crucible of cross-examination.

Antonin Scalia, Associate Justice of the
Supreme Court of the United States

Don't start preparing to cross-examination the defense's medical expert, or any expert, when your trial begins. Begin preparing for the cross-examination of any expert long before trial. I created a system in my office for collecting all materials on all doctors throughout my career, and I keep files on every doctor who has ever rendered a report in one of my cases. In addition, and I cannot stress the importance of this enough, I have relationships with other lawyers who do the exact same thing, and we exchange reports, deposition transcripts, and trial transcripts to create a dossier on every defense doctor.

Additionally, I subpoena financial documents and documents that reflect the amount of work defense doctors perform, what type of work they perform, the amounts they receive, and for whom they perform the exams. This collateral information is a great complement to the medical portion of a cross-examination. I like to introduce the financial and bias evidence first during cross-examination and then attack on the medicine. Some of my colleagues do the opposite—as everyone knows, there are many ways to skin a cat—choose whatever works best for you. Below is a checklist for preparing to cross-examine any defense expert witness:

- ◆ Save all medical reports.
  - » Every lawyer who handles personal injury claims should save every defense report he receives.

- ◆ Create a file for every defense medical expert.
  - » You should create a filing system where each defense expert has his or her own sub file, and save every report from every case. In addition, ask your colleagues for their reports to add to your files.

- ◆ Collect every deposition and trial transcript.
  - » Collect every defense expert's deposition and trial transcripts, and place them in that doctor's sub file.

- ◆ Google the defense medical expert(s) in your case.
  - » You would be surprised what you can find, not only relevant complaints or articles, but even photographs.

- ◆ Obtain a current curriculum vitae.
  - » Many defense doctors' formal education ended before some very relevant technology came into existence. Thus, they have no formal education regarding many modalities

of radiology or other specialties. Also, the year of their board certification will tell you if they were grandfathered in or if they have to get recertified every ten years. Some testifying doctors have not been recertified in forty years.

◆ Search physician databases for licensing, adverse information, and their subspecialty.
  » When googling a defense expert, there are many physician grading sites that can give you information regarding disciplinary hearings or even malpractice suits against the defense doctor. These can be very helpful in cross-examination, but only in certain situations.

◆ Research, know, and understand the medicine.
  » The most important element needed when cross-examining a defense doctor is knowing and understanding the medicine. *No excuses.* You *must* review all of the necessary medicine relevant to your case. Call your experts and have them explain anything you do not understand. Additionally, get all the medical journals, treatises, and test books on the subject and use them to cross the doctor. Make it the defense doctor versus the entire medical community, not just your doctor versus their doctor.

◆ Subpoena all medical reports and invoices from any defense medical exams.
  » Subpoena all medical reports and invoices from the defense doctor or defense medical legal company. If you have every report a defense doctor has written in the last three years and they have never found someone injured, they are toast. Additionally, if they billed over one million

dollars for the last three years and also found no one injured, they are really toast.

◆ Serve supplemental notices to produce in order to obtain
medical reports, invoices, and reports where the defense
doctor found injury.
   » A common tactic I use during discovery is to serve a
   supplemental notice to produce that requests any five
   reports, authored during their career, where they found
   a soft-tissue injury causally related to an accident. They
   typically provide none and give some lame excuse, such
   as they have written thousands and it would be impossible to locate one. You can have lots of fun having them
   explain that answer when you drill down on cross.

◆ Request any medical treatises the defense medical examiner
relied on.
   » Defense doctors typically give generic testimony or cite a
   medical article treatise or book chapter. Obtain every one
   and read them thoroughly. You would be surprised how
   many times the article is in direct contrast to the defense
   doctor's testimony.

There is plenty of information you can obtain from the websites
of defense examiners, their reviews on WebMD,[1] other similar
sites, or even a news article about them. You should perform this
research on all of the defense experts in your community.

   Some attorneys, such as Dorothy Clay-Sims from Florida,
even go as far as calling each and every board, school, or organization the doctors' claim they belong to. They find out what it
takes to be a member and if the doctor actually does belong to the
organization. It can be devastating to a doctor when you know
an organization's membership criteria. When he rants on during
qualification about how he is a distinguished member of such and

1 www.webmd.com

such, during voir dire all you have to do is cross-examine him on the fact that the only criteria to belong to said organization is receive a mailer and pay $300 a year, and every doctor with a license can be a member.

CHAPTER TAKEAWAYS

- Research every defense expert.

- Begin with a Google search.

- Obtain information others have gathered.

- Depose the doctor.

- There is no limit on how much research you can do.

24

CROSS-EXAMINING THE DEFENSE MEDICAL EXPERT'S QUALIFICATIONS

If you confront anyone who has lied with the truth, he will usually admit it—often out of sheer surprise. It is only necessary to guess right to produce your effect.

Agatha Christie

A ttack! Attack! Attack! When the defense calls their experts, you must attack immediately, the first chance you get. That chance is going to come during voir dire when their experts are being qualified to give opinions. When the defense counsel qualifies his expert, he will have the doctor tell the jury what a great and accomplished doctor he is, about being an army surgeon in Vietnam, and how he goes to third world countries in Africa to teach surgeons there the proper techniques for general surgery. The defense counsel will then ask the judge to qualify the expert.

When the judge asks me if I want to examine or have any objections to this doctor being qualified as an expert, I always ask questions that allow the jury to understand that this guy is not as much of an expert as he thinks he is. It's not so much what his expertise is, as it is what it is not. You must expose the areas of medicine in which this doctor has little or no training, yet is giving opinions on in his testimony. If you stand and say "no objection," you admit the doctor is an expert, and his opinion now has credibility.

The orthopedists and neurologists who testify for the defense often do not even have a subspecialty, unlike your client's treating doctor or surgeon. They have often never performed the surgery that is the case's subject matter, and they are frequently too old to have been in medical school during the advent of certain diagnostic tests like MRI scans and PET scans. Their experience reviewing MRI studies is often limited to their forensic work as a defense expert or from attending a seminar. The jury must know this.

I never ultimately object, or seldom ultimately object, to a defense expert's qualifications to being an expert in the case. The last thing I want to do is to argue with the judge about a defense expert's qualifications and have the judge overrule me and tell the jury, in open court, that the witness is indeed an expert. This is straight out of *A Few Good Men*, when Demi Moore's character challenges an expert's qualifications and is overruled by the judge. An expert needs very little experience to be qualified, but it's not about whether they are qualified. It's about how qualified they are.

An orthopedist who was once a general surgeon and has long since retired is clearly not as qualified as a board-certified and Harvard trained neuroradiologist with a two-year fellowship in brain and spine diagnostic radiology to interpret an MRI of the cervical spine. This must be fleshed out during voir dire. After I perform voir dire during a defense expert's qualification, I tell the judge (with a smile on my face) that I have no objection, although my body language will suggest that this expert is not qualified at all.

Here is a typical cross-examination of a defense medical expert on voir dire using no other information than his own CV.

Q: Good morning, doctor.

A: Good morning.

Q: Doctor, you are not a radiologist, correct?

A: No, I am not.

Q: And you are not a board-certified radiologist, correct?

A: No, I am an orthopedist.

Q: And you are not a board-certified neuroradiologist, correct?

A: No, I am an orthopedist.

Q: And you are not even a neuroradiologist, correct?

A: No, I am an orthopedic surgeon.

Q: You cannot enter an MRI facility and draft an MRI report, can you?

A: No, but I can read films.

Q: We will get to that in a moment. And you are not a neurologist, correct?

A: No, I am an orthopedic surgeon.

Q: And you are not a board-certified neurologist, correct?

A: No, I am an orthopedist.

Q: You are an orthopedist, correct?

A: Yes.

Q: Have you done a two-year fellowship in spine surgery?

A: No.

Q: Have you ever been the primary surgeon on a spinal fusion?

A: I have assisted.

Q: I will ask you again. Have you ever been the primary surgeon on a spinal fusion?

A: No.

Q: Doctor, when did you complete your formal education?

A: 1976.

Q: When did MRIs become a reliable modality of diagnostic radiology?

A: The mid eighties.

Q: Thus, you have no formal education in interpreting an MRI?

A: I have attended numerous symposiums and lectures.

Q: Were you graded on your ability to interpret an MRI?

A: No.

Here is another example of a recent voir dire of a retired orthopedic surgeon and how you can use his own CV and prior reports to turn him into toast before he even gets to testify for the defense. This is exactly why you want to collect every report the doctor has ever written. Again, these can be collected through your own practice or by asking your fellow plaintiffs' attorneys for copies that you can all share.

Q: Good morning, doctor.

A: Good morning.

Q: Doctor, I have a copy of your CV here—that's like a resume for professionals, correct?

A: Yes.

Q: And in your education section it says "Education and Medical Training." Your education ends in 1965. It says here, "Hand Fellow, August through December 1965"; does that sound accurate?

A: Yes.

Q: What is a hand fellow? Does that mean you did surgery on hands?

A: I took some extra training in hand surgery, as an elective addition to the program.

Q: Okay. So, there is no hand issue in this case, correct?

A: No.

Q: Okay. Now, it also says here in "Credentials and Licensing" that you were board-certified July 1st, 1969—well, "board certification, ABOS, January 16th, 1969," correct?

A: Yes.

Q: And you said you were grandfathered in, so you didn't have to be recertified every ten years, correct?

A: Since then, yes.

Q: So, in other words—

A: I had to take the test then, but I don't have to take it again.

Q: Yes, you took the test in '69, you passed, but you weren't recertified in '79, right?

A: That's correct.

Q: Or '89?

A: That's correct.

Q: Or '99?

A: Correct.

Q: Or 2009?

A: Right.

Q: And you're not going to be recertified in 2019, right?

A: I'd hope that they don't change the rules by then.

Q: So, in other words, it's been forty-three years since you've been board-certified, correct?

A: Yes.

Q: It's 2012 now, forty-three years have passed. Now, in medicine, actually, the reason they have you get recertified now is because of the advancements in medicine, correct?

A: No.

Q: That's not why they have you get recertified?

A: No.

Q: Okay, why?

[Here is a situation where I do not know what he is going to answer but my gut feeling tells me that no matter what he says or how long he rambles, he will not be able to get out of this one. So, I am breaking the number one rule in cross-examination: never ask a question you do not know the answer to, and the number two rule: never ask an open-ended question. I do break those rules from time to time, but only when I know for a fact the expert will not be able to wiggle his way out of it. This is straight out of Irving Younger's "The Ten Commandments of Cross-Examination." I guess I am a sinner.]

A: Well, I was part—I was on various committees at the time, actually, and there was a very contentious argument. There was a lot of political pressure to have the various boards institute recertification. There was never, to my knowledge, any demonstration that doctors currently practicing had fallen behind. But it was largely a political process.

Q: Because Dr. Opera—you know Dr. Opera, right?

A: I've met him, yes.

Q: He was here and he said he had to be recertified and he said it was because of the changes in medicine and you have to be tested again. That's not true?

Q: Well, that was part of the process when they put recertification in, so I think I'm in a better position than young Dr. Opera to determine what happened at that time.

Q: Young Dr. Opera, who is the Chief of Orthopedics at Woden Hospital?

A: Right.

Q: So, in other words, did you grandfather yourself in?

A: No, I did not.

Q: Okay. Now, you testified, and we looked at—just talked about your resume, the education that ended in 1967, and you testified earlier that MRIs came into existence in the mid-eighties, correct?

A: That's correct.

Q: Plenty of science has advanced since 1967, correct?

A: Sure.

Q: The microwave?

A: Yes.

Q: The cell phone?

A: Uh-huh.

Q: Is that a yes?

A: Yes.

Q: We put a man on the moon *after* you were board-certified, correct?

A: Yes.

Q: Cablevision?

A: Yeah.

Q: The Internet?

A: That is true.

Q: PET scans?

A: Yes.

Q: Robotic surgery?

A: Yup.

Q: Personal computers?

A: Yeah.

Q: Videogames?

A: Yes.

Q: Arthroscopic surgery with fiber optics?

A: Arthroscopy began in Japan in the 1930s. It was perfected in the 1970s.

Q: Knee replacement surgery?

A: Yes.

Q: Doctor, all of the medical advances we just discussed occurred after you were certified, true?

A: Yes.

[I have cross-examined this doctor several times, including a more than four-hour deposition that completely ruined any chance he would ever be successful against me again. He knows what I am going to ask him and had defense counsel attempt to diffuse some of my upcoming questions, including that his education ended before MRIs became an accepted modality of diagnostic radiology or had even been invented for that matter. Despite his attempt to diffuse the situation, I continue to drill down on this topic.]

Q: So, it had been almost twenty years since you had graduated medical school?

A: Yes. More than twenty.

Q: Now under "Education," that ends in 1967, so in other words, you've had no formal training in interpreting MRIs?

A: I think you're skipping more than half of my CV there. I mean, I talked about continuing education courses, annual academy meetings and so forth. It's all in there.

Q: Okay, we can talk about that. Because I know as a lawyer I also have to have continuing education, you are aware of that, right?

A: I'm glad.

Q: CLE, CME, right? You ever hear of that term, "CLE"?

A: No.

Q: Continuing Legal Education. We have the same requirements you have. Now, when you go to these—for these CME credits which you claim are Continuing Medical Education, you sign in when you get there, right?

A: Yes.

Q: And then at the end of the day, you sign out, right?

A: No, I don't think we ever sign out.

Q: So—

A: We turn in a sheet. We rate a course after each meeting. They give us a score sheet and we rate the course.

Q: Okay, you rate the course, but they don't rate you?

A: That's correct.

Q: So, nobody is grading you on whether or not you're accurate in your readings of MRIs?

A: That's correct.

Q: Now, I have a report that you wrote April 17, 2012, ironically to Mr. ...[the same defense attorney in this case] and it says: "I would strongly recommend that the imaging studies from the 2004 accident be obtained and submitted along with the current studies to a board-certified specialist in the field of radiology for the purpose of direct side-by-side comparison." You wrote that?

A: Sounds like me.

Q: So, in other words, you're holding yourself out as an expert, in front of this jury, of interpreting MRI studies, when you actually say, "I would strongly recommend that the imaging studies be compared to other studies." Does that mean you're not qualified—to do a side-by-side comparison?

DEFENSE ATTORNEY: Judge, can I just interrupt? An objection of what this report, what case this is on?

MR. CAPOZZI: Here, it's on a case called *Thistle v. Clover* [fictionalized].

DEFENSE ATTORNEY: So it's not on this case?

MR. CAPOZZI: No.

MR. CAPOZZI: [Back to the defense expert] Correct? You told Mr. ... that he should hire a board-certified radiologist to interpret the films?

A: In this case—

Q: In that case.

A: In that case, I did.

Q: Okay. So, now we had a board-certified radiologist come in here and read the films the other day, on Monday, with—

A: In a different case. Not in that case.

Q: In this case.

A: Yes.

[This is getting like a *Get Smart* episode.]

Q: In this case. So, in other words, you weren't qualified to read side-by-side films of a back surgery?

A: I didn't believe I said in that report that I was not qualified to do it.

Q: Well, it says, "I would strongly recommend." Why would—if you're an expert in the field, why would you need somebody else to come in who is board-certified in radiology?

A: Well, because I occasionally find that with certain attorneys— when there has been a radiology expert, certain attorneys like yourself will tend to do what you're doing now and discredit me, so that there was—in that case there was an attorney—

Q: Because your training is questionable.

A: Excuse me, there was a radiology expert, and I disagreed very strongly with him, and in anticipation of this type of exam— this isn't cross-examination, whatever it is you're doing—in anticipation of this type of questioning, I suggested that you might—it might be to your interest to have a radiologist testify in that matter. I never said that I wasn't qualified, and very often even when I say that, they send me the films.

Q: Yeah, you said, "I would strongly recommend," so in other words, you know that you're not qualified to interpret an MRI film?

A: I just told you that's not true at all.

Q: Okay. So, in other words, okay, you did interpret MRI films in this case, right?

A: Yes, I did.

Q: In fact, you're going to do a side-by-side comparison today, aren't you?

A: I think—well, it depends on what questions I'm asked, yes.

Q: Okay. You're going to take the films from the 2009 accident and you're going to take the films from the 2010 accident, right? And you're going to show this jury, right?

A: If I'm asked to, yes.

Q: And you're going to disagree with the board-certified radiologist?

A: I don't see any major disagreements.

Q: Did you agree with the radiologist who read the films?

A: I have to go through the whole reports again. Basically, I don't think either of us saw any herniations or any significant injury.

Q: No, he saw a bulge. He saw a bulge at C-3/4, C-3/4 and C-5/6, and he also saw a bulge at L-3/4. And are you going to testify that those things exist?

A: Probably.

Q: Okay, we'll see what you say. But didn't you say there is a disc ridge complex?

A: I have to look at these again to see exactly what I said, what I described. But these are a lot of terms that are overlapping, so when we look at the films, I will tell you what I see.

Q: Okay. So, in other words, if you agree with him, why do you have to show the jury the films?

A: Because the defense counsel would like me to.

Q: Okay. So, we're going to see what you say. We're going to see whether or not you agree with his findings, okay? Now, you testified earlier that in 1998 you did your last surgery?

A: That's correct.

Q: And then you said "I stopped doing surgery in '98," right?

A: Correct.

Q: You also stopped seeing patients, didn't you?

A: I think I testified probably before you, as well, that I see an occasional—I've always said 99 percent of what I do is this. I have some old patients. They understand that we no longer have x-ray in the office, and that I would no longer be doing any surgery if they needed it. I do see an occasional very few patients for consultations and second opinions, who are not involved in litigation.

Was that fun or what? This is exactly the type of circumstance we see all the time. Thousands of litigants have lost their right to be compensated for serious injuries because their attorneys failed to obtain the information needed to effectively cross-examine a defense medical expert.

This is why every plaintiff's attorney must join their state trial lawyers association, join that organization's listserv, exchange information with their brothers and sisters, and attend seminars with local and national speakers that will teach them these types of effective cross-examination tools. If you are not a member of the American Association of Justice (AAJ) and your state association of justice you are committing legal malpractice. It is that important.

CHAPTER TAKEAWAYS

◆ During the qualification of a defense expert, never offer the phrase "no objections, Your Honor."

◆ Attack the defense expert immediately on what specialties he is not (or barely) qualified to render opinions on.

◆ Never object to an expert not being qualified in a certain area of medicine if he has some or minimal experience in that field. It is not too difficult to be qualified on a subject matter if you have some experience. Cross the doctor on the weight of his qualifications.

◆ If you want to knock an expert out completely, request a 104 hearing outside the presence of a jury.

◆ Join organizations like the AAJ and your state plaintiff's association.

25

A Reasonable Degree of Medical Probability
Cross-Examining Defense Medical Experts

In cross-examination, as in fishing, nothing is more un-gainly than a fisherman pulled into the water by his catch.

Louis Nizer

Medical experts must testify to a reasonable degree of medical probability. Possibility is not enough. Anything is possible. A reasonable degree of medical probability means 51 percent and is consistent with the preponderance of the evidence standard of proof. Thus, if you have to prove a case by a preponderance of the evidence, your doctors' opinions must be that the accident *probably* caused the injuries to the plaintiff. If so, you have a *prima facie* personal injury case. However, the jury must determine if your doctors' opinions are more credible than the defense doctors' opinions. This is the battle of the experts.

Cross-examining the defense medical experts is the most exciting aspect of a trial. The defense doctor is often the only hurdle standing in the way of you proving your medical case since liability is stipulated in many automobile accident cases. Therefore, a successful cross-examination of the defense medical expert is crucial.

A reasonable degree of medical probability is based on the patient's diagnosis. Doctors must take into account all of the elements needed to make a diagnosis, including history, complaints, diagnostic tests, and the physical exam findings to determine causation and prognosis. As discussed earlier, the history and the onset of pain can often tell a doctor what happened and what injury occurred to the body part. Before there were MRIs or more sophisticated diagnostic tests, physicians only had their physical exam findings and the patient's history and complaints to render a diagnosis.

The advent of MRIs and EMGs not only enabled physicians to confirm their diagnoses, it also spawned some deceptive defense tactics. Prior to the advent of sophisticated diagnostic testing, the defense doctors would just claim the patient was a malingerer, exaggerator, or faker. Now in addition to calling our clients liars, they can try to deceive a jury because a percentage of the population has preexisting soft-tissue degeneration, including bulges, herniations, and wear and tear on the knees and shoulders. Despite this percentage being less than probable, after the deceptive defense doctors testify that one third of the population have preexisting herniations and bulges, they brazenly say it is more likely to a reasonable degree of medical probability that the findings were preexisting—regardless of the fact that the math is against them.

You must expose this. They have cost thousands of injured people, entitled to monetary compensation for injuries they sustained due to the negligence of others, to lose in a courtroom because a plaintiff's trial attorney was not prepared, or informed on how, to defeat them. Well, the party is over for them, or should be if attorneys take the time to learn the medicine, share information with other attorneys from the plaintiff's bar, and believe in the cause they are fighting for.

You must believe in your case. If it is not a great case, do not try it. I have heard so many lawyers tell me in the hallways, when asked how their trial is going, that they are going to lose. The case sucks, the plaintiff sucks, their doctor sucks. You cannot go into a courtroom feeling despair. A jury will smell it on you.

Defense doctors notoriously ignore the history and onset of symptoms. I once sprained my ankle during a trial while carrying garbage cans full of mulch on my property. I stepped on a rock and twisted my ankle. It hurt so much I had to stop working.

I was summing up the next day and, during my summation, I decided to tell the jury about my experience the day before. I mentioned how I hurt myself, and that I knew how I hurt myself because the pain started at the exact moment I stepped on that rock and my ankle twisted. I told them that if a doctor examined me and told me I had "degeneration of the foot" I would laugh in his face. I knew how I got injured, and any doctor worth his salt could figure it out.

The defense doctors in that case had claimed that, although my client had been in an accident, the pain began at the moment of the accident, and the diagnostic tests and physical exam findings had confirmed the injuries, the damage was degenerative. That is their testimony in every soft-tissue case.

The following is the cross-examination of a neurologist who attempted to claim my client's injuries were degenerative in nature, despite no evidence of degeneration at all. There is medical literature that completely debunks this argument, and although I did not cross the doctor on the actual literature in this case, this cross was based on medical literature I knew the doctor had quoted in his report but did not cite.

Q: Okay. Now, this next—this is what I want to talk to you about: "similar changes can be described, even in clinically asymptomatic individuals." So, are you telling this jury that there's a percentage of the population that has preexisting bulges?

A: That the—that has them?

Q: Yes. Asymptomatic people.

A: Yeah.

Q: How many? What's the percentage?

A: Oh, the reports vary, at least in terms of the herniations. But, it's described from 20 percent to 50—60 percent of people.

Q: What are you—

A: Bulges—bulges—I don't know the exact numbers. They're probably higher than that, but I don't know the exact number.

Q: Well, what are you basing that on?

A: Basing it on medical reports—which I don't know any specific in mind—medical reports, and—and in clinical experience.

Q: So in other words, every time somebody comes in and has a bulge that was asymptomatic you record it somewhere or are you really basing it on some medical literature?

A: No. It's not a specific record—I don't accumulate numbers, however, of what those disc bulges are, but it's just in looking at films. There you have multiple levels in an MRI. And there may be one symptomatic level L5-Sl. And there's certainly bulges in L2-L3, L3-L4 which are not the problematic ones.

Q: You ever hear—

A: We do MRIs for other reasons also. We see bulges there too, for the—for—for tumors and other diseases in the spine. We certainly come across bulging as well.

Q: Now, have you ever heard the premise that a third of the un-injured population is walking around with herniations and disc bulges? Have you heard that term?

A: A third?

Q: A third.

A: I don't know the exact number. I wouldn't be surprised if somebody said it.

Q: Okay. Now, you also know that bulges are more prevalent with people's age as they get older?

A: It's true. Yes.

Q: You would expect to find more bulges in a fifty-year-old than a twenty-year-old, correct?

A: Take—take all the fifty-year-olds and all of the twenty-year-olds, percentage-wise I'll see more of those as they get—a person gets old.

Q: In fact, have you ever heard of this? That 20 percent of twenty-year-olds have bulging discs? 50 percent of fifty-ear-olds—curve that goes like that. Have you ever heard that? 60 percent of sixty-year-olds, 70 percent of seventy-year-olds, and the older you get the more—the more probable you're going to have a bulging disc. You ever hear of that?

[I draw the diagram below while I cross-examine this witness.]

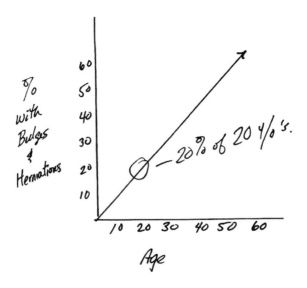

A: If I—I don't remember the exact number or the line you're drawing, but the numbers of—say of 20 percent in the twenties that could have bulges or protrusion. And in going up I wouldn't be surprised if numbers are tossed around in that—that—that range.

Q: So, that's in the ballpark, right?

A: It's—it's in the ballpark. But I'm sure it's been quoted as longer and I'm sure it's been quoted higher as well.

Q: Okay.

A: But it exists.

Q: Well, let me ask you a question. You're here talking and you're here testifying to a reasonable degree of medical probability, correct?

A: Correct.

Q: And that's something that's more probable than not, medically speaking?

A: Correct.

Q: So, in other words, if something was 51 percent, you'd say it's medically probable, right?

A: Medically probable for what?

Q: Anything, because we're talking about probabilities. So something that's 51 percent as opposed to 49 percent, 51 is more probable than 49? You get it? It's math.

A: Yeah. It's math, but I was just thinking in the—in the medical aspect of it. What's more—something more probable to happen or something more that was to exist?

Q: Well, everything you're saying—you said—you testified to a reasonable degree of probability right? Let me ask you, everything you give is to a reasonable degree of probability.

A: Right.

Q: So, if 20 percent of twenty-year-olds probably have a disc bulge, isn't it true that 80 percent of them do not?

A: That—that probability of the existence of the bulge, that's what you're asking.

Q: Yes.

A: Oh, I'd say that—that the—the—you said 51 percent, but I—I think you meant the 20 percent. Yes. The—most of the people would not have a disc bulge.

Q: Exactly. So, that's four times more likely they don't have a disc bulge, right?

A: Correct.

Q: So, isn't that more probable than somebody having a preexisting condition?

A: These are—

Q: It's just simple math, doctor. You said that 20 percent of the people have a bulging disc. Yet, you said that my client's bulge is probably not related to this accident, because it's preexisting—it's probably preexisting. All your opinions are to a degree of medical probability. In fact, you said, "Ms. Castillo has a normal neurological examination. There are no objective findings of permanent neurological injury or dysfunction in connection with her symptoms as a consequence of the motor vehicle accident on February 13, 2007."

A: Okay.

This doctor testified that a twenty-year-old had a preexisting bulge despite it being four times more probable she did not. The diagram I drew during this cross works well with clients forty-nine years old and under. There are many articles regarding degenerative disc disease that support this diagram and others that support the premise that even persons forty-nine years old and older probably didn't have a preexisting bulge or herniation. It is much easier to prove a herniation in a younger person was caused by an accident than a bulge in older persons. When an older person only has a bulging disc, I often argue an aggravation of an asymptomatic preexisting condition because preexisting bulges are prevalent in older people and bulging discs and a degenerated spine are more susceptible to injury.

Here is another fun example of a defense spine surgeon testifying at a deposition to a reasonable degree of medical probability and not realizing he is proving my case for me. Although he cites a medical textbook chapter that claims 28–35 percent of the population has preexisting asymptomatic disc herniations, he will not admit that 65–72 percent do not.

Q: Doctor, if I had 100 marbles on this table and 28 of them were red and 72 of them were black, and we put them in a jar and I stuck my hand in the jar, what would I be more probable or likely to pull out, a red marble or a black marble?

A: Which are the black, 70 percent?

Q: 72 blacks.

A: So you would be more likely to pull out a black marble.

Q: Okay, and if there were 35 red and 65 black what would I probably pull out?

A: Still, most likely a black.

Q: In fact it's almost twice as likely I would pull out a black one, correct?

A: I agree.

Q: In the first example I gave you it's probably three times more likely I would pull out a black one, right?

A: I agree.

Q: So if between 28 and 35 percent of people have a herniated disc, then doesn't that mean 65 to 72 percent do not?

A: That's not what I said, so I am going to read you what I said.

Q: No, no, no, no.

A: That's not what I said.

Q: I know what you said because I have been sitting here listening to you for two hours, and let's talk math, because you took math in order to become a doctor, right?

A: I did.

Q: And 65 plus 35 equals 100, right?

A: I agree.

Q: So if 35 percent of people have a herniated disc, doesn't it make sense, mathematically, that 65 percent do not?

A: No, that's not what I said.

Q: What did you say?

A: I said 28 to 35 percent of disc herniations occur in the absence of symptoms. That's what I said.

Q: So then the other 65 to 72 percent occur with symptoms?

A: We don't know. I can only—I can only tell you what the textbook says.

Q: So, in other words, you can always fall back on the position that there is a 35 percent chance that someone has a preexisting herniated disc, right?

A: That is generally accepted—that is correct and it would not be from this textbook; there are other articles that show that herniations are common in the population.

Q: And one of them would be the Boden article. Are you familiar with that one?

A: If that's from the *New England Journal of Medicine*, that might be the one.

Q: It's actually from the *Journal of Joint and Bone Surgery*. And now what's your understanding of what that article says?

A: I think my best recollection, since it's been twenty or fifteen years ago, is that it was 28 percent. But there are some other articles that had less and some more.

Again, by testifying that 28 to 35 percent of the population has an asymptomatic preexisting disc herniation, the doctor is really testifying that 65 to 72 percent of the population does not, thus proving my case by a preponderance of the evidence—51 percent. In my closing, I explained to the jury that I must prove my case by a preponderance of the evidence, by 51 percent, or what is more likely. Not only had my doctor's testified to a reasonable degree of medical probability, the defense doctors had proven my case because, by their own testimony, it was two to three times more likely that my client's disc herniation was not preexisting.

I recommend everyone read the Boden article in the *Journal of Bone and Joint Surgery* because it states that 20 percent of the asymptomatic population between twenty through sixty have a preexisting herniated disc.[1] The article further breaks things down by the disc level herniated and by the age of the patient. You would be surprised how helpful this article is on cross-examination. For example, the percentage of preexisting herniations in a thirty-five-year-old woman at L3-L4 is about 4 percent. Thus, it is twenty-five times more likely the herniated disc was not preexisting.

You have to make the case about their doctors versus the entire medical community, not their doctors versus our doctors. The medical literature supports our position, enabling us to make this argument. I have incorporated this idea into every one of my trials.

There are several articles that deal with MRI scans of the lumbar or cervical spine in the asymptomatic population. You have to read and understand the medical literature, speak with experts, and know the medicine. When you know the medicine, you can challenge the defense medical experts head on and disprove the deceptive practices and BS they spew in court every day. You absolutely have to show that their opinions are not the opinions of the medical community. When coupled with the collateral attack regarding income and bias, a deceptive defense medical expert stands no chance in a courtroom.

1 Scott D. Boden MD, et al., "Abnormal Magnetic Resonance Scans of the Lumbar Spine in Asymptomatic Subjects," *The Journal of Bone and Joint Surgery* 72 (March 1990): 403–408.

CHAPTER TAKEAWAYS

◆ A reasonable degree of medical probability is more than 50 percent.

◆ When the defense doctor's opinions are based on statistics that are less than 50 percent, they cannot be probable.

◆ The diagnosis of an injury is based on the patient's history, symptoms, diagnostic testing, and physical exam findings.

◆ The history will typically tip the scales of probability into the favor of the plaintiff, absent any prior accidents and injuries.

26

THE COLLATERAL ATTACK
Cross-Examining Defense Medical Experts

Revenge is a dish best served cold.

Pierre Choderlos de Laclos

Many lawyers feel the collateral attack on a doctor's income is unnecessary and counterproductive. They feel that eliciting how much money a doctor earns performing defense exams only proves he is worth the price because of his expertise. I understand why they feel this way, but I do not agree. In my experience, it can be very effective when coupled with the medical opinions doctors give at trial.

If you can show that the money they earn is a factor that biases their opinions, then you should do it. I have always believed that if you can get a jury to understand what is occurring on the defense side of the case, exposing the deceptive defense practices as clearly as you see them, you will win the case. What the defense examiners are doing is obvious and clearly unworthy of any credibility. We must show the jury the doctor's obvious bias and then cross-examine them on the medicine. If we have the knowledge to cross-examine the doctors and the information on their finances then this should be a cakewalk. The following is a cross-examination of a defense orthopedist regarding the income he earns from performing defense examinations:

Q: Doctor, when did you start performing these defense examinations?

A: I'm not sure. I first started seeing some people in the 1990s. If you're asking me when I started doing defense exams set up by CFO, it's 2003. I cannot remember the exact date.

Q: And you perform these exams to supplement your income?

A: I receive reimbursement for them, yes.

Q: And one-third of your entire practice is dedicated to these exams?

A: Approximately one third of my practice is dedicated to performing independent medical exams, and about half of those exams are set up by CFO.

Q: Is it one-third of your time, or one third of your income?

A: One third of my time.

Q: Is it one third of your income?

A: Probably a little more than that.

Q: Doctor, how many of these defense examinations do you perform a week? And I don't mean only for CFO, I mean the exams you perform in New York and the ones you also do in New Jersey.

A: It varies from day to day and week to week. For CFO, I see people Monday mornings actually.

Q: Okay.

A: And that would be anywhere from four to eight exams.

Q: Can we use the number six? Would that be safe to say?

A: Six is fair.

Q: Now Ms. Beck, you examined her in the evening right?

A: Yes, one Monday a month I examine people for CFO in Passaic in the evenings.

Q: Okay, so how many people do you exam a month, not only for CFO, but for all defense exams?

A: For CFO, probably twenty-five to thirty a month. But that varies from month to month.

[At this point I began to write out the number of defense exams the doctor performed per month. I then multiplied it by the amount of money he charged per exam and then added in all of the other defense oriented items he charged for. I wrote this on a flip chart on an easel and identified it as something like "Doctor Wurst: Defense Income." As you are about to see, the good doctor wanted to see what I was writing and asked me so.]

Q: Okay.

A: Can I see that?

Q: It's actually for the jury to see, but maybe I can turn it a little so you can also see. How's that?

A: That's fine.

Q: So thirty a month for them.

A: And then when I go to New York its about five times a month, probably forty exams a month.

Q: Okay, then that's seventy defense exams a month?

A: Yeah probably, yes.

Q: And when you perform the exam, do you generate a report?

A: Yes.

Q: Okay and how much do you charge for a defense exam and report?

A: For CFO, I get remunerated $200.

Q: Remunerated? What the heck is that?

[Laughter]

A: I charge $200. I do not know what CFO charges.

Q: So if that's thirty exams a month at $200 a piece, then you make $6,000 a month performing defense exams for CFO, correct?

A: Yes.

Q: And then you do another forty a month for whom?

A: A company called Stetson and Garder.

Q: And how much do you charge for those?

A: $140 each.

Q: So that's forty times $140, or $5,600, sound right?

A: Yes.

Q: So that's $11,600 per month performing defense exams and drafting an initial report, correct?

A: Sounds about right.

Q: Do you work twelve months a year?

A: I do.

Q: So lets multiply twelve by $11,600. So you earn $139,200 a year just performing defense exams and writing initial reports?

A: That may be a little low.

Q: How low is it?

A: Probably more in the 150–160 range.

Q: Okay, but we are not finished yet. How many times a year do you testify in court?

A: Approximately six.

Q: All for the defense?

A: Yes.

Q: How much do you get paid?

A: $1,500 per half day.

Q: Ever go a full day?

A: Not yet.

Q: You may today, doctor. So that's another $9,000 a year for court appearances. Now let's discuss record review and film review and the drafting of supplemental reports, okay?

A: Sure.

Q: How many supplemental reports do you write per case?

A: Sometimes, none.

Q: And other times, several, correct?

A: Yes.

Q: Do you draft more than fifty per month?

A: No.

Q: More than twenty?

A: Yes.

Q: How about thirty?

A: That's in the ballpark.

Q: How much do you charge per supplemental report?

A: For record review or film review, approximately one hundred dollars.

Q: So, it's thirty per month times one hundred dollars and that equals $3,000 per month, and then times twelve months, and that equals $36,000 per year for supplemental reports, correct?

A: Yes.

Q: Now how about depositions. Are you deposed as a defense expert?

A: Yes.

Q: How often?

A: About two times per month.

Q: For twelve months?

A: Yes.

Q: How much per deposition?

A: $1,000.

Q: Okay, times two times per month, times twelve months equals $24,000?

A: Yes.

Q: So, doctor, adding up all of these items, it appears you perform 840 exams per year, 360 supplemental reports, come to court six times a year, and get deposed twenty-four times a year, and all that totals to $208,200, seem right?

A: Sure, could be a little more, could be a little less.

Q: How long have you been doing defense exams at this rate?

A: About fifteen years.

[I then went over to the board and, without talking, multiplied fifteen by $208,200 and wrote out the total. In this case, I wrote $3,123,000. I then continued to question the defense doctor.]

Q: Does that amount of money per year cause you to sway your opinion in favor of the defense?

A: Not at all.

Q: You realize that if you opine favorably toward the plaintiff, any plaintiff, then you do not get deposed, do not come to court, and are not remunerated for this income. Do you realize that?

A: I am asked to examine someone and then give my opinion. I am compensated for that opinion.

Q: Doctor, can trauma cause a disc to herniate?

A: Yes, of course.

Q: All of the 840 people you examined last year experienced some sort of trauma, correct?

A: Yes, that is true.

Q: Did you find a herniated disc related to any of those traumas?

A: I don't recall.

The table below illustrates how much Dr. Wurst earns per year performing defense work, including the total amount of money he has earned in the last fifteen years, over $3 million.

DR. WURST DEFENSE INCOME

Monthly Income from Defense Exams
30 exams x $200 each = $6,000
40 exams x $140 each = $5,600
Monthly Total: $11,600
Total Yearly Income from Defense Work
12 months x 70 exams = 840 defense exams per year
12 months x $11,600 = $139,200
6 in court testimonies x $1,500 = $9,000
360 supplemental reports x $100 = $36,000
24 depositions x $1,000 = $24,000
Yearly Total: $208,200
Total Earned over the Past Fifteen Years: $3,123,000

After I cross-examined this expert, the case settled. This was the case where my son James was born later that day. I think the collateral attack had a lot to do with the settlement. Unfortunately for the reader, the body language and demeanor of the witness cannot be seen while reading these transcripts, but I can assure you it did not help the defense. Whether this tactic works and whether the verdict will be higher because of it is yet to be seen. I have heard jurors say they felt the retired defense doctor had paid his dues and deserved to charge all that money. I have also heard the jurors call the defense doctor a slimeball. I think in a vacuum just crunching the numbers with these defense doctors is useless. You still have to show how their opinions are not valid.

CHAPTER TAKEAWAYS

- If you do not know the amount of defense work an expert performs, then take his deposition to determine it prior to trial.

- Make sure to write out the amounts an expert earns by category, reports, exams, film and record reviews, no-show appointments, depositions, and trial testimony.

- Calculate the amount a defense expert has earned by year and over the course of his career.

- Remember, presenting a defense expert's income is meaningless without exposing the deficiencies in his opinion.

27

CROSS-EXAMINATION
OF A DEFENSE DENTIST

Trips to the dentist—I like to postpone that kind of thing.

Johnny Depp

I was never a big fan of TMJ (temporomandibular joint) cases. But these injuries are common following a motor vehicle accident. Just like the cervical or lumbar spine, the temporomandibular joints can be displaced and damaged due to whiplash or a direct blow to the face. Just like with degenerative disc disease when it comes to the spine, the defense dentists use similar arguments.

Their favorite argument is that a TMJ disc derangement cannot occur without a direct blow to the face. They don't consider an air bag deploying with the force of a shotgun blast a direct blow to the jaw. They consider that a soft impact. I often cross-examine them with the premise that if I placed my face into a sink full of water, then the water would be soft; but if I dove off the George Washington Bridge, the impact to my face wouldn't be so soft would it? How can they possibly opine that an air bag deploying in your face is a soft impact?

Some of the defense dentists in New Jersey are worse than the defense orthopedists and neurologists when it comes to disputing the medicine that is supported by the entire medical community, or in their case, the entire dental community. Their second favorite argument is that the client grinds their teeth, or what is known as *bruxism,* and that is the reason for their pain and discomfort after the accident. Bruxism causes a serrated knife like pattern on the tongue, so if they see this so-called serrated imprint on your client's tongue they immediately claim bruxism is the cause of the problem, and not the airbag that exploded into the plaintiff's face.

In one particular trial, a notorious defense dentist, who is at least eighty-five years old, opined that my client had no clicking or popping in her jaw. Not only could you see her jaw joints distort with your eyes, the clicking could be heard from across the room. As I discussed earlier, I'd had this client schedule a follow up visit with her treating dentist three days after the defense exam. In the follow up, her treating dentist recorded that her jaw clicked. Before the defense exam, her treating dentists and oral maxillofacial surgeons—and there were four—all recorded clicking during their examinations, diagnosed her with TMJ disc derangement, and recommended surgery. They also all causally related the injury to the motor vehicle accident.

Despite the findings of five dental experts, this defense doctor had the audacity to opine that my client had a normal exam, that there was no clicking, and no causal relationship to the accident. During the trial, I had lunch with my client the day before this defense dentist was going to testify and we were discussing her jaw. When she opened her mouth I could hear the clicking and even see her jaw distort. I wanted the jury to hear this. I began to think of my three-year-old son, who wanted to be a doctor that week and was running around the house in his doctor outfit and toy stethoscope. I told my client I was going to bring in that toy stethoscope and have the defense dentist and jury listen to her jaw. She said she worked in a medical office and could bring in a real stethoscope. As much as I wanted to bring my son's toy stethoscope to court to prove you could even hear it with a toy, I decided to use the real one.

The following day, when I had the expert on the stand, I asked him if he heard any clicking during his examination. He testified he did not. I then asked him if jaw clicking was indicative of disc derangement in the TMJ. He said it was. I then whipped out the stethoscope.

Over the objection of defense counsel, the judge agreed to allow me not only to have the defense expert listen to my client's jaw sounds in front of the jury with the stethoscope, but to also allow each juror to listen as well. My argument was that if a client has a visible scar you want the jury to see, the judge always allows the jury to use their visual sense to determine the severity of the scar. I argued this was the same, but we were allowing the jury to use their audio sense to hear the severity of the clicking.

I sat my client down in a chair and asked the good doctor to listen and tell the jury if he heard clicking. He listened and stated he did not hear anything. I then had the jurors come up to the witness stand area one-by-one and, using the stethoscope, listen to my client's jaw when she opened her mouth. We even brought alcohol wipes to clean the stethoscope prior to the next juror listening. The judge ordered the jury not to make a statement or act in any way that would indicate if they heard it or not.

The following day, the jury came back with a verdict for my client after deliberating for twenty minutes. It was priceless. Although I do not have the transcript of that cross-examination, I do have a section from my summation in that case regarding the stethoscope.

Summation

Now let's talk about the jaw. There are two ways to prove permanency or injury through objective medical evidence. One is diagnostic testing, like we did in this case with the MRIs and all the other tests ordered by Dr. Weaver. The second is through objective evidence on physical exam.

Dr. Featherman has seen this woman since April of 2007 until the present day. He sent her to four different surgeons. They all recommended surgery on her jaw. They all say she needs surgery.

Dr. Featherman said even if she did have surgery, she would still only regain 70 percent of her jaw function back. She can't eat. She's afraid to yawn. She cannot sleep. Yelling, talking on the phone, talking for long periods of time, all of these things bother her. If I could not eat, I would be dead.

So, Dr. Featherman says, right away, I hear clicking and that's indicative of a displaced disc in the jaw. [He] sends her for physical therapy. That doesn't help. She is still having problems. He orders an MRI, but the MRI comes back normal. He said, "there are many other objective signs of injury on physical exam, including the clicking sound." So there was a second MRI performed. She went for a second MRI. That one was positive.

Dr. Munsterman had that MRI. Did you hear one peep out of him about it? Never said a word. He couldn't explain that one away. In fact, I said to him, "Dr. Featherman and the other four surgeons all said she had clicking." Some of them examined her before Munsterman, some after Munsterman.

He examined her for five minutes, "heard nothing" he said.

So I asked him, "if there was clicking what would that indicate?"

He says, "a displaced disc."

So I said, "let's see if you hear a clicking now." So, we let him listen for it with the stethoscope.

He said "no," he doesn't hear it. Maybe he just can't hear. He is kind of elderly. Maybe he can't hear.

DEFENSE COUNSEL: Objection!

THE COURT: Just continue, he is what he is.

MR. CAPOZZI: So …

THE COURT: I don't know how old he is.

MR. CAPOZZI: So, I don't know, I don't want to call him a flat-out liar.

DEFENSE COUNSEL: Objection! He called him a liar.

THE COURT: He said he doesn't want to call him a liar. Overruled.

MR. CAPOZZI: Thank you, Your Honor. I don't want to call him a liar, so maybe he just really can't hear it. But, you know right after he did it, I asked all of you to listen. So, it is what it is. You know he should be able to hear a sound like that. It's there. It's there. So, think about how credible he is.

So, the jaw, we know she has a displaced disc. It's clicking. And you know, the sad part is she's in a tough spot. She is stuck between a rock and a hard place. She's been trying to get this surgery, her insurance ran out. She missed three weeks from work after the accident and lost her job. [She] got another job, went right back into the work force. She's a student too. But she had no health insurance. Now, she finally gets health insurance, and they claim her jaw injury is preexisting and they won't pay for it.

[This trial was in 2012, prior to the Affordable Care Act.]

New Jersey Rule of Evidence 411 states that you cannot mention or insinuate that the defendant has liability insurance. This is one of the simplest but most misunderstood rules in the State. There are several judges and defense attorneys who believe that this rule applies to all insurance, including health insurance. Thankfully, the judge in the case above knew the law and allowed me to speak about it during the trial.

I always have the Rules of Evidence with me at trial and often have to use the book at sidebar to recite the law to the judge. I think this mutation of the rule has been argued for so long that even a great jurist may believe it actually is the rule. This is just an example of why we should always read (and reread) the rules of evidence and of court. Each time I reread them I always have an "Aha!" moment.

The rules also have notes that explain rulings from other cases with various fact patterns. If you have the book with you at sidebar, you can show the judge the case law and it will be difficult for him to overrule you when the law is right there in black and white. This can be done very respectfully using the correct tone and approach.

With regard to Rule 411, the spirit of the rule is not to insinuate that the defendant has insurance coverage, because if a jury knew the defendant had deep pockets it would be prejudicial. That has nothing to do with whether a client could not get treatment because their insurance ran out or they had no health insurance.

Chapter Takeaways

- Injuries to the temporomandibular joints are real and can occur from whiplash or a blow to the face.

- Just like when cross-examining a defense orthopedist, you must learn the dental medicine to effectively cross-examine a defense dentist.

- You must know the anatomy of the body part you are dealing with, including the jaw and face.

- Whenever possible, utilize simple ways to prove your case, like the stethoscope example.

28

CROSS-EXAMINING MEDICAL EXPERTS WITH THE LITERATURE

The only real lawyers are trial lawyers, and trial lawyers try cases to juries.

Clarence Darrow

Not only can we cross-examine defense doctors on their qualifications, income and bias, and the medicine, we can also cross-examine them with the medical literature.

The medical literature supports our position. Yet defense doctors typically argue that the literature supports the presence of a preexisting condition. There is a clear example of how to deal with this in chapter 22, "Objective Medical Evidence." Knowing the medical literature, really knowing it, can be lethal to defense medical experts. I always have certain medical articles and book chapters in my trial bag and use them when necessary to cross-examine defense doctors.

There are several articles that relate to magnetic resonance imaging of the spine in asymptomatic individuals. They are specific to regions of the spine and in several authoritative journals. The articles the defense most frequently cites, or miscites, are the 1994 *New England Journal of Medicine* article by Jensen[1] and the 1990 *Journal of Bone and Joint Surgery* article by Boden.[2] Defense experts often testify that a percentage of the uninjured population, regardless of age, have preexisting degenerative disc diseases, including herniated discs. They'll argue that bulging discs are a normal finding in every age group. The articles I am about to reference prove that not only is it less probable for a person of almost any age to have a preexisting asymptomatic herniated disc, but that bulges are not normal and can be caused by trauma.

Absent trauma, disc herniations are rare. In fact, common sense dictates that most, if not all, injuries can be traced to a single event. Think about this simple preposition:

A person gets in an auto accident. She goes to the emergency room with excruciating pain in her neck. Her tests are negative for fracture and she is sent home. She wakes up in worse pain and goes to see her primary care physician or local chiropractor, complaining of pain since the accident a day or two before. He treats her conservatively, but her pain does not cease.

After a month, she decides she should get some diagnostic testing performed to rule out a herniated disc.

1 Maureen C. Jensen MD, et al., "Magnetic Resonance Imaging of the Lumbar Spine in People Without Back Pain," *New England Journal of Medicine* 331 (July 1994): 69-73.

2 Scott D. Boden MD, et al., "Abnormal Magnetic Resonance Scans of the Lumbar Spine in Asymptomatic Subjects," *The Journal of Bone and Joint Surgery* 72 (March 1990): 403–408.

Her tests come back positive for herniation. The EMG is positive for acute cervical radiculopathy. Her pain continues and she is referred to a pain management doctor who gives her three epidural injections, which give her temporary relief. Her pain returns, so she gets a surgical consult. In the meantime a lawsuit is filed. Three years go by and the pain is still unbearable. She gets sent to the defense doctor who examines her for five minutes and opines that the injury is preexisting because a percentage of the population has asymptomatic herniated discs.

As a trial lawyer, if you can argue the above scenario effectively enough to show a jury how ridiculous the defense argument is, you will win. It is that simple. In the worst-case scenario, you claim the accident aggravated a latent condition. On cross, the majority of defense doctors will admit an asymptomatic degenerative condition can be aggravated by trauma. I always use this as a fall-back position. The Jensen article is an excellent source for debunking the typical defense argument that states a third of the population has asymptomatic herniations absent trauma.

This article studies ninety-eight individuals and is broken down by lumbar spine level and age group. Not only can you cross-examine the defense doctor on the prevalence of disc abnormalities in your client's age group, but also on the prevalence of abnormalities on the level of the spine where you client was injured. The article concludes that although bulges increase with age, herniations do not. It is very important to understand the tables in these articles. The subjects of the Jensen study range between twenty to sixty or so. The Boden article on the cervical spine studies individuals between ages twenty and seventy-three. Both of these articles allow you to plug your client's age and injury into a formula.

For example, if my forty-one-year-old client has a herniated disc at the L4-L5 level, table three of the Jensen article details the levels of the spine, the age groups of the people studied, and the percentage of those with bulges, protrusions, or extruded herniations. According to this article, which the defense always relies upon, only five out of twenty-three subjects between forty and forty-nine had a disc protrusion at L4-L5. The percentage of preexisting disc protrusions at the L4-L5 level in a forty-one-year-old is around twenty percent. Thus, it is four times more probable that the disc herniation or protrusion was not present prior to the accident. With these percentages, how can a defense doctor claim an injury is more likely to be preexisting? How? They just do. And many plaintiffs' lawyers are not armed with the literature to shove it right back from where it came.

There were several medical articles written regarding MRI scans on asymptomatic individuals in the early nineties. I can only speculate that the insurance companies were trying to come up with some ammunition to counter the number of back injuries and their costs on the work force, and for the purposes of defense litigation in automobile accidents. If I were a gambling man, and I am, I would bet that the insurance industry was behind the funding and research of these medical articles. I say this because they came out in spurts around the same time and quote the medical costs for treating these types of injuries.

In addition to the Jensen article, two very important articles I use often are "Abnormal Magnetic Resonance Scans of the Lumbar Spine in Asymptomatic Subjects" in the *Journal of Bone and Joint Surgery*[3] and "Abnormal Magnetic Resonance Scans of the Cervical Spine in Asymptomatic

---

3 Scott D. Boden MD, et al., "Abnormal Magnetic Resonance Scans of the Lumbar Spine in Asymptomatic Subjects," *The Journal of Bone and Joint Surgery* 72 (March 1990): 403–408

Subjects" also in the *Journal of Bone and Joint Surgery*.[4] These articles are frequently referenced, but not exactly cited, by defense doctors. They claim there are studies that show a percentage of the population has preexisting findings. Whenever I question the name of the article, they can never recall. I then ask if it is the *New England Journal of Medicine* or *Journal of Bone and Joint Surgery* articles and they often say, "yeah that's the one."

The Boden cervical article is very helpful to plaintiffs' attorneys. Of the sixty-three subjects who were studied, 10 percent of those under forty had a herniated disc and 5 percent of those over forty had a herniated disc. This is hardly the 33 percent the defense doctors claim. Despite the less than overwhelming evidence of preexisting disc herniations, the article concluded that predicating operative decisions on diagnostic tests without precisely matching those findings with clinical signs and symptoms was a dangerous practice. This conclusion also confirms the importance of the history section of the diagnosis and that MRIs cannot be read in a vacuum. The Jensen article also concludes that, "MRI examinations can be meaningless if considered in isolation."[5]

This conclusion is very important in cases where the defense calls a radiologist who, without reviewing any of the clinical findings, opines a disc herniation was preexisting based on the MRI findings alone. This should be an *in limine* motion as radiologists, in their everyday lives, do not opine regarding the age and cause of disc herniations or bulges. It is outside the scope of their expertise. They are simply asked to interpret the findings of the MRI, not to diagnose the cause of the patient's condition or injury. However when they come to court for the defense, they

---

4 Scott D. Boden MD, et al., "Abnormal Magnetic Resonance Scans of the Cervical Spine in Asymptomatic Subjects," *The Journal of Bone and Joint Surgery* 72 (September 1990): 1178-1184

5 Maureen C. Jensen MD, et al., "Magnetic Resonance Imaging of the Lumbar Spine in People Without Back Pain," *New England Journal of Medicine* 331 (July 1994): 72.

attempt to opine that the degeneration, including the herniations or bulges themselves, was preexisting.

Degeneration, to some degree, is always going to be present on an MRI scan. Do not try to run away from it. Embrace it and argue that although there is some expected degeneration, the patient was pain free and only after the accident became symptomatic. Moreover, while you may have diffuse degeneration or desiccation at all levels of the spine, there are not herniations or bulges present at every level. This proves you can have degeneration or desiccation without herniation or bulge.

The defense doctors also argue that bulges cannot be caused by trauma. This always puzzled me. Why does trauma have to cause the annulus of a disc to tear completely through, causing a herniation, and not tear partially, causing a bulge? It makes no sense. It would make perfect sense that a lighter impact would cause a slighter tear, thus causing a bulge.

I often use the "pothole" argument for this premise. I am driving down the highway at 50 mph and hit a pothole. The tire blows out and I crack my rim. The next day I am driving down the highway and knowing that the pothole is there slow down but hit it anyway. Instead of blowing out my tire, I notice a bubble on the side of it.

Less of an impact causes less damage. I still have to buy a new tire regardless. The Boden lumbar article clearly states that disc bulges, which had previously been thought to be caused by degeneration, can also be caused by trauma:

> The sensitivity of magnetic resonance imaging also enabled us to study the incidence and distribution of bulging and degenerated discs. In addition to the surprisingly high prevalence of those findings in asymptomatic subjects of all ages (twenty-years-old or older), the interrelationship of the two findings differed from what had been expected. Although many

authors have considered bulging of a disc to be caused by degeneration, in our asymptomatic subjects only half of the degenerated discs bulged, and only half of the bulging discs were also degenerated. In addition, in the older subjects, the prevalence of degeneration was more increased than that of bulging. These relationships may suggest that factors other than degeneration result in bulging.[6]

There are also numerous articles and book chapters on TMJ and whether there must be direct trauma to the mandible in order to suffer a traumatic TMJ injury. One such book, the recognized textbook authored by Kaplan and Assael can be found on the shelves of the defense dentists who argue against it. In a recent *de bene esse* deposition, Jay Kimball from my old office cross-examined the same Dr. Munsterman I used the stethoscope on in the dentist's own office. Right behind the doctor on his shelf was the Kaplan book. Jay cross-examined him on the book and whether it was an authority. Jay even pointed out to him that the book was right behind him on his own shelf. However, the good dentist testified that although the text is relied upon by dentists in the field, he did not agree with the book. he does not coun

The book has an entire chapter on whiplash and TMJ: chapter 11, "Structural alteration of the TMJ occurs in a rear end collision."[7] There are also illustrations of a whiplash injury and its effect on the TMJs in a rear-end collision.

Plaintiffs' lawyers must read and understand the medical literature. For cross-examination, there is no substitute for knowing the medicine and being able to defend yourself when the doctor

6 Scott D. Boden MD, et al., "Abnormal Magnetic Resonance Scans of the Lumbar Spine in Asymptomatic Subjects," *The Journal of Bone and Joint Surgery* 72 (March 1990): 403–408.

7 Andrew S. Kaplan and Leon A. Assael. *Temporomandibular Disorders: Diagnosis and Treatment*, (Saunders, 1991): 202.

turns the cross on you. I have seen many a doctor, cross-examined by a lawyer who is out of his league, stretch the truth and get away with it because the plaintiff's lawyer did not understand the medicine or have the medical literature to shut the expert down.

The cross-examination of defense experts is typically the last part of any trial and the last witness to be called in the defense's case. The next step is the closing argument where the domino demonstration takes place and where the plaintiff's lawyer gets to tie everything together.

CHAPTER TAKEAWAYS

◆ Read the medical articles that relate to your case.

◆ Read the medical literature thoroughly, and understand it in detail so you can effectively cross a medical doctor with research in his specialty.

◆ Use either *in limine* motions to limit the testimony a defense expert will attempt to get in or a 104 hearing outside the presence of the jury.

◆ Use the diagrams and charts within the articles to clearly display to the jury what these articles actually mean.

29

SUMMATION

A jury consists of twelve persons chosen to decide who has the better lawyer.

Robert Frost

In my summation, I tell the jury that I promised them in my opening I would prove all the necessary elements of my case. The first thing I do is pull out the diagram I drew during my opening and go back over it now that the evidence is in.

1. THE △ WAS PROBABLY NEGLIGENT.

2. THE △'S NEGLIGENCE WAS PROBABLY A PROXIMATE CAUSE OF THE ACCIDENT.

3. THE △'S NEGLIGENCE WAS PROBABLY A PROXIMATE CAUSE OF THE INJURIES.

4. THE INJURIES ARE PROBABLY PERMANENT.

I then discuss the accident and the negligence of the defendant. In the *Jones v. Smith* case, the defendants did not stipulate to negligence. I first address element number one, which is "the defendant was probably negligent."

1. THE △ WAS PROBABLY NEGLIGENT.

With regard to the accident, I go back to the diagram of the intersection I drew in my opening. I reiterate that, had the defendant just stopped and carefully looked both ways before proceeding into the intersection, we would not be here. Mrs. Jones would have continued to work and never experienced all of the injuries, pain and suffering, and painful treatment—including undergoing several epidural injections under anesthesia, and surgery. She would have continued living her life the way she was, enjoying the activities she enjoyed doing, and working pain free at the job she loved.

The defendant's failure to act reasonably by looking both ways was negligent. We only need to prove her failure to act reasonably was probably negligent. She was definitely negligent. However, I do not want to give you the impression that the proving of negligence is easy, it is not.

The typical juror drives an automobile and is familiar with driving. When the defendant has rear-ended your client, or taken a left turn into your client, or failed to carefully proceed into an intersection, the jurors will understand that those things are negligent. But do not gloss over it as if it is a given.

I have made this mistake and been tagged for 49 percent negligence by a jury where the defendant crossed over the double-yellow line and struck my client head on. The defense had an accident reconstructionist who I thought I had rendered useless on cross-examination, but the jury obviously felt otherwise. You can never be thorough enough when proving negligence. Nothing is a given.

You are probably asking "where was his accident reconstructionist?" I had retained one. However, he was unavailable and the judge refused to adjourn the trial. So, I went ahead without him, as I assumed I would easily prove the case without him. I did win the case and received a decent award for my client, but I still got tagged for a large percentage of negligence.

I often hire accident reconstructionists and biomechanical experts in my cases. When I have a minor impact, soft-tissue (MIST) case with serious injuries and barely any visible property damage, I often hire a biomechanical expert to either prove that a low impact collision can cause serious injuries or to disprove the defense expert's opinion stating the opposite. However, it may not always be cost effective to prove negligence—but that's my next book. After proving that the defendant was probably negligent, I then discuss element number two.

2. THE △'S NEGLIGENCE WAS PROBABLY A PROXIMATE CAUSE OF THE ACCIDENT.

If the defendant had not carelessly entered the intersection, then no accident would have occurred. All she needed to do was look carefully both ways and not assume there was no one coming down the road. If she had taken those extra two seconds to survey the roadway, she would have seen the plaintiff's vehicle and not pulled out into the path of the plaintiff. But for the negligence, the accident does not occur. I reiterate that although we only have to prove probabilities, there is no doubt that the defendant's negligence *was* the cause of the accident.

PROVE YOUR CASE USING MATH

During my summation, after I go through the client's timeline and argue causation of injuries, but before I get to the domino theory demonstration, I speak about the standard of proof and the preponderance of evidence standard. I explain again, as I did in my opening, that we are speaking about probabilities, about what is more likely: the 51 percent standard. I then continue by stating that I told the jury I would prove my client's case by at least a preponderance of evidence in my opening, and in fact I did so. Even if they believe the defense medical experts, the defense medical experts proved my case for me.

I remind the jury that during both direct examination and cross-examination, the defense experts testified that the reason they believed Mrs. Jones's injuries were preexisting was that a percentage of the population has preexisting degenerative disc disease. They wrote in their expert reports the day they examined Mrs. Jones, months, or in some cases a year, before they reviewed the actual MRI films, that because a percentage of the uninjured population has preexisting degeneration and herniated discs, the injuries were not caused by the accident. The percentage the experts quoted was one-third of the population. I asked them if "one-third of the uninjured asymptomatic population has these preexisting disc herniations, then two-thirds do not, correct?" It was a simple math question. They reluctantly answered "yes." Thus, even if the jury believes them, I have proven the case by 67 percent, much more than the 51 percent I needed.

The fact of the matter is, the very research the defense experts rely upon to formulate these opinions is even more damning to their testimony. The medical literature states that, between the ages of twenty and sixty, only 19 percent of the population has a preexisting herniated disc. That means that they proved my case for me by 81 percent.

It is four times more likely the disc herniations in Mrs. Jones's cervical and lumbar spine were not preexisting. In fact, when the literature they cite in their reports is broken down further, it states that of the study participants in Mrs. Jones's age group, the forty to forty-nine age group, only 9 percent had a preexisting asymptomatic disc herniation. That means 91 percent of people in Mrs. Jones's age group do not have preexisting herniated discs.

The truth of the matter is, the defense proved my case for me to the tune of 91 percent. It is more likely, if you believe the defense, that Mrs. Jones's herniated discs were caused by the accident. Mrs. Jones has proven her case by a preponderance of the evidence. Not only do Mrs. Jones's doctors all agree the herniated discs were caused by the accident, the medical community would agree as well. The literature proves it.

During direct examination, I asked the treating doctors who properly took into account all the pieces that create a diagnosis, if they had an opinion within a reasonable degree of medical probability. They naturally testified yes, and that because of the lack of a prior history of injury to the body part, the complaints, the onset of symptoms, the diagnostic testing results, and the findings on their physical examinations, they not only felt the injury was probably caused by the accident but they felt strongly about it. "How strongly, percentage wise?" I asked. They often responded 95 to 99 percent. Radiologists, when testifying, often state their opinions to 100 percent.

If you think about it, radiologists are not testifying that a herniated disc is probably present on the MRI scan. They testify it is there, period. It's 100 percent. Although it is not proper for a radiologist to testify that a herniated disc was caused by trauma (it is outside the scope of their expertise absent clinical correlation), they are often able, on cross-examination, to debunk the defense attorney's theories of preexisting herniations being caused by degenerative disc disease. The radiologist's typical answer should be "it is very rare," which, based on the literature is true. I then incorporate that response on cross into my mathematical calculation.

I then write the responses from each of the testifying doctors into my mathematical equation for the jury and write out all the percentage of probabilities responses of all the doctors. I add the responses up and average them out for the jury and tell them I have proven the case by 88 percent based on the evidence elicited at trial through the testimony of all the doctors. The diagram below is how I write these figures out during closing before the jury.

CAUSATION: TREATING DOCTORS

- Dr. Maggiano: 95 percent

- Dr. Vesper: 90 percent

- Dr. Lee: 90 percent

- Dr. James: 95 percent

Causation: Defense Doctors

- Dr. Wurst: 91 percent

- Dr. Goldberg: 67 percent

Total Average: 88 percent

Mrs. Jones proved that the defendant's negligence caused the injury by 88 percent. That is far in excess of the 51 percent she needed to prove her case by a preponderance of the evidence. Remember, the permanence of your client's injury has been agreed upon by every doctor, even the doctors for the defense. So it's the causation of the injury that is the main issue in every soft-tissue case.

CHAPTER TAKEAWAYS

- Be sure to request a specific percentage amount from your client's treating doctors, based on your client's history.

- Use medical literature against defense experts.

- Make the math easy for the jury.

30

PICASSO AND DAMAGES

My mother said to me, "If you are a soldier, you will become a general, if you are a monk, you will become the Pope." Instead, I was a painter, who became Picasso.

Pablo Picasso

Like I said earlier, my thoughts on damages are different than most attorneys. The chronological story of the case, as it unfolds and sets up the domino theory, also includes damages. If the defendant's negligence does not occur, then the damages that come afterwards do not occur. I have read numerous books that say trial lawyers should spend at least 50 percent of their time talking about damages in opening and closing. I disagree for the following reasons:

I spend very little time talking about damages. I do spend lots of time speaking about the accident, injuries, and the plaintiff's pain and suffering. However, I never mention money. The jury knows why they are there. In New Jersey, we have a rule called the *time unit rule*. Although we can ask for actual economic damages, we are not permitted to ask the jury for a specific amount of money for pain and suffering. But we can give the jury some guidance through the time unit rule.

The time unit rule must be dealt with very carefully, because on a soft-tissue case a jury could feel you are over reaching if you break down the pain and suffering damages into hours, minutes, or seconds. The time unit rule allows you to ask the jury to use time as a measuring stick for damages, including life expectancy. For example, if someone is going to live for ten years, you could break it down into 120 months, 520 weeks, 3,650 days, 87,600 hours or 5,256,000 seconds of pain and suffering.

The idea is to throw out the largest number you can to allow the jury to multiply it times whatever amount of money someone should be awarded, like $500 an hour for 87,600 hours over the next ten years. You also have to deduct the amount of time the plaintiff sleeps, such as eight hours a day. Therefore one could argue that their client suffers sixteen hours a day, seven days a week, twelve months a year times ten years. In a soft-tissue case, unless it's the most severe, I would be very careful not to offend jurors by throwing out huge numbers like those mentioned above. I never do that.

I use it a different way, and this is another reason plaintiffs' attorneys must work together and share information. I got this idea from a seminar I did not even attend. Jay Kimball, the attorney from my previous firm who I mentioned earlier, attended a seminar titled "Utilizing the Time Unit Rule" and called me from the seminar. He said Wade Suthard, the lecturer and a fellow NJAJ board member, had a great idea regarding damages. It was about Picasso and help wanted. I listened and loved it. I now use it in every trial. Some of the best ideas are ideas you borrow from another lawyer. Thanks, Wade. The following is an example of one of my closing arguments in an elevator case using the Picasso and damages method:

In the American civil justice system, when someone gets injured because of the negligence or carelessness of another, compensation is the only award you could possibly give them. You can't take them back to February 26, 2009, and say "you're back to normal." It's impossible. But what we can do is compensate people with money, as much as that will ever do anything for them. It will never make them whole. I mean this family was destroyed. And I know that sounds cliche-ish, but it's true.

Now when it comes to damages, and you heard my adversary say I was going to do something or say something about awarding money per hour, per minute, per second—that's called the time-unit rule. I'm not going to do that at all. I am going to make it easier. Oh, by the way, there are 11,500,000 reasons why Mr. Galpern testified.

[I am referring to the defense liability expert's income over the past twelve years as I am flipping through the various charts I drew during the trial. I was searching for a blank page to write out this argument I was about to make and came across the page where I questioned the liability expert about his income from doing defense work and thought I would throw that one line out there regarding same.]

But there's something called the time-unit rule and I think everyone in their own lives already uses this stuff so you may be familiar with what I am about to say. Some people get paid yearly salaries, some people get paid hourly, some people get paid per day, some people get paid biweekly, monthly, in all different forms.

That's all this is. When you consider damages, think about it as awarding a salary for everything Mr. Thomas has been through up until today. From the date of the incident, February 27, 2009, until today, which is May 15, 2013. So more than four years have passed since this incident. But then not only after today, Mr. Thomas is fifty-years old right now. The life expectancy of a fifty-year-old man in New Jersey is 30.3 years. The judge is going to instruct you that you can consider the life expectancy of Mr. Thomas. So he has to be compensated from the date of the accident up until today. And, if you think he's got an injury that's going to last into the future and damages that last into the future for 30.3 more years, you can also award him future damages. He might live longer. He might live less. We don't know. But that's the average. So how do you figure that out? And when we just talked about jobs and things like that.

If there was a Picasso painting in the elevator with Mr. Thomas and it broke in half during this incident, I could bring fifty experts in here, from all over the world, to say that painting's worth $4 million, $5 million, or that painting's worth $10 million because it's something that they could value.

This tactic is like walking a tightrope. The law states you cannot argue to a jury a specific figure for pain and suffering. By making the Picasso argument, you are not suggesting to the jury what the pain and suffering of the plaintiff is worth only what some piece of art is worth. I have made this type of argument several times without any objection ever from my adversaries. I did have a judge tell me in chambers that she thought it was out of bounds, but I disagree.

There is also a rule in New Jersey called *the golden rule.* The golden rule says we cannot ask the jury to place themselves in the shoes of the plaintiff. What would you want if this happened to you? If we violate the golden rule, it's a mistrial. I have read several books of very prominent lawyers whose states must not have the golden rule, because they constantly say, "Imagine this happened to you." So, we must be very careful not to suggest money or break the golden rule, it's very hard to make these arguments without breaking one or the other. The closing argument continued:

> But there is no measuring stick to value human life. Humans are not artwork. Humans are men and women. There is nothing like that. There is nothing. There's nothing. And the only guidance I can give you, you already have. It is your own life experience and you know the function of money and you know what pain and suffering is like.
>
> These are the damages he's asking for: pain and suffering, disability and loss of enjoyment of life, and impairment. The judge is going to instruct you on these damages. He certainly suffered these things.
>
> Now, I read the papers all the time. I always look at the classifieds, and if there was a help wanted advertisement, and it said "Temporary Job: February 27, 2009, through May 15, 2013," and it said this job entails getting in an elevator on the twenty-seventh floor of Newport Towers, experience the sensation that the elevator is free falling, fear your impending death, stop suddenly with a crash that is described by tenants of the building as an earthquake, get knocked to floor and be unable to move, be lying next to a strange woman on the floor screaming because her leg is broken in three places, it's pitch black, the elevator is swaying, and you are not sure if the elevator is going to break loose and plummet the rest of the way to the ground below, surely killing you.
>
> You think of your family, your kids, your wife, your parents. You lay there waiting for what seems like eternity. Then you hear voices: it's the fire department.

The elevator starts to slowly move upward until the doors are pried open and the light shines through the crack in the door, dust from 10,000 years is now visible floating down like snow upon you.

You are removed from the elevator on a back-board, and wheeled to a waiting ambulance. You are in excruciating pain, go to the hospital, get x-rayed, discharged home, where you vomit, begin physical therapy, see orthopedists, spine surgeons, treat with doctors for over a year, have a life-altering surgery, be afraid to get in an elevator for the next four years, that you can't even go to work anymore because your office is on the twenty-seventh floor and its too high to walk up and down the steps several times a day.

It's hard to imagine when you do go back to work in September that you have to go back on this elevator that crashed, that sounded like an earthquake. And you've got to get back on that elevator and go up to your office, which is just steps from the elevator banks that you can see from your desk chair, from your seat, and do this for the rest of your life.

So it's going to cost you your family, no more sports, no more wrestling with your kids, no more skiing or bowling, no more softball league, no more scratch golfer, no more anything. Just lots of medication, depression, divorce, and lose your kids and the life you knew. Then go to trial for two weeks, get called a liar, lazy, and treated like you are looking for a hand-out. That you are looking for money. What would this job pay? What would the salary for four years be for that job?

I either write out a classified ad like below as I state all of the job duties or I have a preprinted classified ad that looks like it is from the newspaper, describing the duties that are required for the job.

HELP WANTED

TEMPORARY JOB: FEBRUARY 27, 2009–MAY 15, 2013

- Free fall in elevator
- Fear for your life
- Crashing halt
- Excruciating pain
- Ambulance
- Hospital
- Painkillers
- Surgery
- Physical therapy two years
- Continued pain
- Depression

- No more activities, sports, golf, bowling, or baseball
- Divorce
- Lose custody of children
- Move from your home to an apartment by yourself
- Lose your job of twenty-seven years
- Boredom
- Four years of pain

FOUR YEAR SALARY: $ _____

I then discuss the second phase of damages:

> Then there's a second job from May 16, 2013, through September 2043, for 30.3 more years. That's going to last the rest of your life, crashing into things with your car because you can't turn your neck when driving properly, waking up every day in pain, taking Tylenol, taking Advil, taking hot showers to be able to move your neck, and pain and suffering for the rest of your life for thirty more years. But remember what the doctor said? He said 20 percent of people who have that fusion or that disc replacement, that metal disc—you know when you're made you have seven discs in your neck and the weight of your body is distributed over those seven discs. You take one out and put a piece of

metal in, now all the extra stress goes to the remaining six discs, gets distributed unevenly, and it causes problems there. Those levels above and below wear out faster and before you know it, you are experiencing pain, and you need surgery on one or more levels of your cervical spine.

These are things he's going to have to deal with in his old age. He's only fifty, and he's in pretty good shape, svelte-wise, and that's where it ends.

But, ladies and gentlemen, what Schindler, and I'm only going to talk about Schindler to be quite honest with you, I'm not that concerned with the building. I'm concerned with them because they're the ones who are responsible for those elevators, and they are the ones who didn't maintain those elevators, and they are the ones that caused this incident and they are the ones that made Ralph what he is today—they put him in the condition he's in today.

So thank you very much for your time. Although this person, this couple, have been my responsibility for the last four years, I'm now handing that responsibility over to you, because I've done everything I could for them. Now I'm handing that responsibility over to you to take it the rest of the way… for the next 30.3 years. Thank you.

Next is the second wanted ad I either have preprinted or I draw on the fly. Everything I am discussing was either testified to by the plaintiff, his coworkers, children, ex-wife, or treating physicians, including the surgeon who performed surgery on his cervical spine.

HELP WANTED

PERMANENT JOB: MAY 16, 2013–MAY 15, 2043

- Pain
- Pain killers
- Future surgery
- Live alone
- Backing into things with your car
- No job
- Depression

- Still not more activities, sports, golf, bowling, or baseball
- Divorce
- Children grow up
- Grow old by yourself
- Boredom
- Thirty years of pain

THIRTY YEAR SALARY: $ _____

You must be careful in a smaller case not to overreach regarding damages. I just do not feel comfortable breaking down damages to days, hours, minutes, and seconds. And who knows, that might just be me.

In my opinion and from my own experience, when you start throwing numbers out to the jury like: "Ms. Jones is going to live for 3,560,000 minutes and she should be compensated for every one of those minutes," I have seen jurors roll their eyes. I am just not comfortable arguing numbers like that in a soft-tissue case with minimal treatment and minor property damage. What I have done, in cases where I think the jury is on the edge because the plaintiff was not a good witness, is downplay damages and just try to win the case. The jury usually rules in my favor but gives a modest award. There are many ways to handle arguing damages, and everyone must argue them the way they are most comfortable. However, by using the domino theory and chronologically connecting the damages to the accident, you should be able to prove your damages were proximately caused by the negligence of the defendant.

CHAPTER TAKEAWAYS

◆ If the case is substantial, and the law allows it in your state, use a time-unit or life-expectancy analysis to maximize damages.

◆ Compare the human body to something valuable, as the human body is the most valuable object on earth.

◆ Be sure to recreate the incident and the fear and chaos associated with it, as that experience is also a damage caused by the defendant's negligence.

◆ Be sure to write out all of the activities your client enjoyed prior to the accident, and what he is left with following the accident.

◆ Create your own way to argue damages that you are comfortable with and that reflects the value of the case.

31

DISPROVING THE DEFENDANT'S CASE

Belief makes the way for confidence, and it is confidence that paves the way for clarity of vision, and clarity of vision experiences the success.

Anil Sinha

The next step after arguing damages in summation is to disprove the defendant's case. One day in my office, I was playing with my dominos and lining them up on my desk, practicing the closing argument for one of my trials when my colleague, James Kimball, walked in and out of the blue said, "You should take out the negligence and collision dominos and show degeneration was not the cause of the accident and injuries." It was brilliant. Not only could I now prove my case but I could also disprove the defendant's case even more convincingly. James's idea was essential to the success of the domino theory.

During your closing, walk over to where the first three dominos were placed and re-iterate what degeneration is: the wear and tear of life on the soft tissues of the body. Remind the jury that the defense is claiming that this is what caused Mrs. Jones's pain and suffering, and not the defendant's negligence. But if the negligence and accident never occur, what happens? We are not here.

I further elaborate that if you believe the defense's argument that degeneration was the proximate cause of Mrs. Jones's pain and suffering, then without the negligence and collision Mrs. Jones still would have gone to the emergency room that day. She would have continued to treat with all of her doctors and gotten the injections and surgery, and would still be in pain today, despite never having experienced pain in the injured body parts or treated with a doctor in her life for those body parts during the 14,000 or so days before the accident. It is key, and I cannot stress it enough, that throughout the trial you must embrace degeneration, because the reality is, it is present and possibly a preexisting condition that made your client more susceptible to injury.

Take away the negligence and collision dominos, numbers two and three, and knock over the degeneration domino, and nothing happens. Only the degeneration domino falls. Tell the jury that without the negligence, without the collision, without the air bag deploying, Mrs. Jones would have continued slowly and painlessly aging. What other explanation is there for a woman who lived 14,000 plus days on earth and, up until one split second before this accident, never saw a doctor for her neck, was never involved in an accident, never suffered from a sports related injury, never had neck pain, and never filed a lawsuit. There is only one reason we are all here: the negligence of the defendant.

Proving the Plaintiff's Case

Immediately following this demonstration, put the negligence and collision dominos back in place and walk down the line of dominos, discussing each one again:

> But in this case there was negligence, and there was a collision. The air bag did deploy, striking Mrs. Jones in the face. She had the immediate onset of pain—the ambulance arrived and took her to the ER. She followed up with her chiropractor, got an MRI, an EMG, consulted with a pain management specialist, got epidurals, went to see an orthopedist—the pain continued, she got surgery, and we are here today, and she will be in pain for the rest of her life.

Return to the beginning of the dominos and discuss the definition of proximate cause. I read it verbatim from the jury charge, knock over the first domino that states "negligence," and watch it set in motion the fall of each of the other dominos, thus demonstrating proximate cause.

Chapter Takeaways

- Use the dominos to not only prove your case but to disprove the defendants theory of a preexisting asymptomatic condition.

- Be sure to read the proximate cause charge from your state just prior to knocking over the negligence domino.

32

DOMINO THEORY
DEMONSTRATION ONE:
Auto Accident

*Vietnam was a lie but at least there was a political agenda.
It was the domino theory.*

Donald Sutherland

The last thing I do in my summation is the domino theory demonstration:

Ladies and gentleman, I'm going to prove the defendant's negligence was the proximate cause of the accident and injuries using this simple demonstration. I am also going to disprove the defendant's argument that my client's injuries were caused by a preexisting degenerative condition.

If there is an issue of degenerative disc disease or preexisting condition, which there always is whether someone is sixteen or ninety, begin with this simple demonstration. For this scenario, the first domino you place should state "degeneration" or the preexisting condition. If you go to www.ccdominos.com, you can see the video demonstration of how I actually perform the domino theory.

Auto Accident: Simple Demonstration

[Place domino one on the jury rail.]

Degeneration

1. Domino One: Degeneration
» Discuss that everyone, beginning in their late teens, begins to suffer some wear and tear and that this plaintiff is no different. Everyone on earth has some degeneration, whether mild, moderate, or severe. This degeneration, or wear and tear, does not mean there was a disc bulge or herniation present.

But for the negligence of the defendant, such as the running of the stop sign, this slowly developing and painless process probably would have continued without incident.

[Place domino two on the jury rail.]

2. Domino Two: Negligence

» The defendant looks down to pick something up off the seat and takes his eyes off of the road.

[Place domino three on the jury rail.]

3. Domino Three: Stop Sign

» The defendant runs the stop sign.

[Place domino four on the jury rail.]

4. Domino Four: Collision

» The accident occurs.

[Place domino five on the jury rail.]

5. Domino Five: Airbag
» The Airbag deploys, striking the plaintiff in the face.

[Place domino six on the jury rail.]

6. Domino Six: Immediate Onset of Pain
» The plaintiff suffers from the immediate onset of neck pain (pain they've never before experienced).

[Place domino seven on the jury rail.]

7. Domino Seven: Ambulance
» The ambulance arrives.

[Place domino eight on the jury rail.]

8. Domino Eight: Emergency Room

» The plaintiff is taken to the hospital, complaining of neck pain.

[Place domino nine on the jury rail.]

9. Domino Nine: Chiropractor

» The plaintiff begins treatment with their doctor.

[Place domino ten on the jury rail.]

10. Domino Ten: Continued Pain

» The plaintiff's pain continues.

[Place domino eleven on the jury rail.]

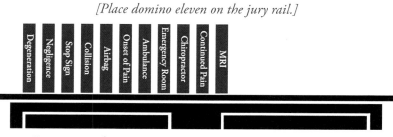

11. Domino Eleven: MRI
» MRIs of the cervical spine are recommended and performed.

[Place domino twelve on the jury rail.]

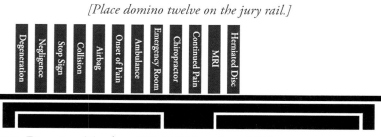

12. Domino Twelve: C5-C6 Herniated Disc
» The plaintiff is diagnosed with a herniated cervical disc.

[Place domino thirteen on the jury rail.]

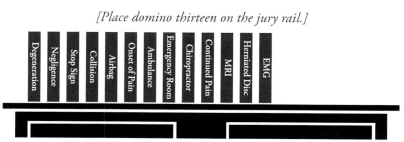

13. Domino Thirteen: EMG
» The plaintiff consults with a neurologist who performs an EMG that confirms the injury is acute.

[Place domino fourteen on the jury rail.]

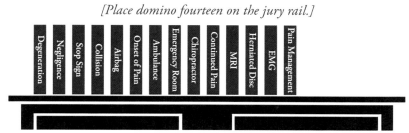

14. Domino Fourteen: Pain Management

» The plaintiff is referred to pain management.

[Place domino fifteen on the jury rail.]

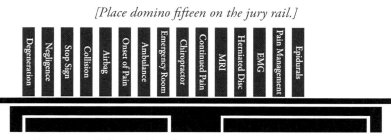

15. Domino Fifteen: Epidurals

» The plaintiff has three epidural injections.

[Place domino sixteen on the jury rail.]

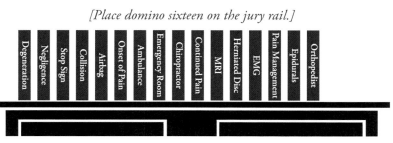

16. Domino Sixteen: Orthopedist

» The plaintiff has some relief but the pain returns. The plaintiff sees an orthopedist.

[Place domino seventeen on the jury rail.]

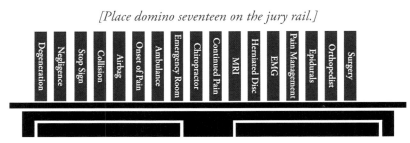

17. Domino Seventeen: Surgery
» Surgery is performed.

[Place domino eighteen on the jury rail.]

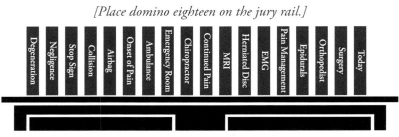

18. Domino Eighteen: Today
» The plaintiff still has complaints four years following the accident.

[This is a great place to insert dominos regarding damages such as: loss of income, out of work for nine months, outstanding medical bills, cannot lift her child, weight gain from lack of exercise, and so on. Use the individual damages in your case to extend the chain of dominos. In a recent trial I set up twenty-seven dominos that included all of the damages my client suffered as a result of the defendant's negligence.]

[Place domino nineteen on the jury rail.]

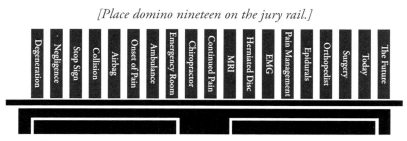

19. Domino Nineteen: The Future

» The plaintiff will live for thirty-two more years. The injuries caused by this accident will not only last from the time of the accident, they will last into the future and probably worsen.

That is the typical sequence of events I use when I utilize the causation dominos in my summation. In a typical case, the defense doctors claim my client has a preexisting degenerative disc disease. They do it in almost every case whether someone is fourteen or ninety-four. When this occurs, use the example above or on my video at www.ccdominos.com. First, you disprove the defense's case, then you prove your case.

[While I am editing this book, I am in Napa, California working with trial strategist Rodney Jew and graphic artist, Amy Gallaher Hall on a police-shooting case. I showed Rodney and Amy the video of the domino theory and Rodney wanted a set overnighted to him so he could examine the dominos. The following day, they started to come up with some great ideas to improve the dominos and the theory. Rodney suggested making the negligence domino red with yellow type and Amy suggested using lowercase letters instead of all caps. We toyed around with a few other ideas but in the end, we decided to only go with those two. I think they are great ideas and I will probably utilize them in the creating the next run of dominos.]

In the following case, my client was twenty-years-old and was in a serious motor vehicle accident. The defense, surprisingly, did not argue the existence of a degenerative disc disease or degeneration. What they argued in this case was that my client suffered a sprain/strain and her MRI of the cervical spine was normal. The treating or reading radiologist interpreted my client's cervical MRI to reveal a disc bulge at C5-C6. Although I have had defense doctors disagree with a positive MRI containing a disc bulge and call it a normal MRI, there is often some desiccation or spurring associated with that disc. I also often see defense doctors call a herniation a bulge. That is a common defense tactic because they then go on to argue that bulges cannot be caused by trauma and are purely degenerative in nature.

Auto Accident: Actual Case

Here is an actual domino theory demonstration from a case where the client was twenty-years-old and the defense claimed her MRI was normal. Because they did not argue degeneration, I started off with domino two, negligence:

> So, ladies and gentlemen, I just want to show you one more thing. What is proximate cause? One of the things, the only thing we need to prove in this case was that her injuries were proximately caused by the accident.
>
> Now, proximate cause is a cause that sets in motion a natural and continuous sequence of events. So, in other words, when the defendant went through the stop sign, she caused the accident, airbag deploying, immediate onset of pain, emergency room, doctors, doctors, doctors, tests, tests, tests, tests. So, did that negligence set in motion all of these things?

Well... they admitted they were negligent. The accident occurred because of that negligence. She got struck in the face with the airbag, there was an immediate onset of pain. She went to the emergency room. She went to the chiropractor. She went to her family doctor. She had shoulder pain, he sent her to an orthopedist. She went to see the TMJ doctor. She continued to have pain and discomfort in her jaw, in her neck, in her back. She got an MRI that was positive in her neck. She got an EMG; it was positive at the same level the disc was bulging. They recommended surgery on her jaw. She continued to have pain. And here we are today. And she has one more for the future because once these injuries are here, they are not going away. So, did this negligence set in motion a natural and continuous sequence of events?

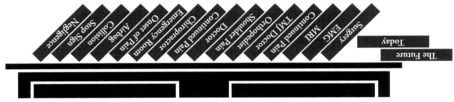

MR. CAPOZZI: Makes perfect sense ladies and gentlemen.

When the jury came back quickly, I thought I was going to lose as quick verdicts almost always spell doom. However, the jury did in fact give a plaintiff's verdict and in just twenty-two minutes. There were no questions, no "can you redefine proximate cause?" The domino theory worked. And the jury had a fun experience at the same time.

Since that case, I have received several verdicts using the domino theory, and every time the verdict was reached quickly, without the need for the judge to redefine proximate cause. When you mention a proximate cause in your opening, use the term with your doctors on direct, explain what a proximate cause is to the jury in your summation, and then show them what it is using the domino theory. They will never ask the judge to redefine it again.

33

DOMINO THEORY
DEMONSTRATION TWO:
Premises Liability

Ashes to ashes, we all fall down.

Jerry Garcia

Just like in an automobile case, a medical malpractice case, or a fall down case, I use the same opening statement and summation format. In my closing argument, I tell the jury that I promised them in my opening I would prove all the necessary elements of my case. The first thing I do is pull out the diagram I drew during my opening and go back over it now that the evidence is in. I also discuss the usual degeneration defense and disprove it. For a premises case, I use the following dominos:

Premises Liability Demonstration

[Place domino one on the jury rail.]

1. Domino One: Degeneration

» Just as with an auto case, I discuss that everyone, beginning in their late teens, begins to suffer some wear and tear, and that this patient is no different. Everyone on earth has some degeneration, whether mild, moderate, or severe. This degeneration, or wear and tear, does not mean there was a disc bulge or herniation present.

But for the negligence of the defendant, such as allowing a dangerous condition to exist on their property, this slowly developing and painless process probably would have continued without incident. The defendant allowed a cracked, raised section of sidewalk to exist on his property for an extended period of time.

[Place domino two on the jury rail.]

2. Domino Two: Negligence

» The defendant, despite numerous complaints, or constructive notice of the raised sidewalk slab, allows a dangerous condition to exist. This should be proven through expert testimony of an engineer or architect.

[Place domino three on the jury rail.]

3. Domino Three: Dangerous Condition

» The expert opines that the raised slab was a dangerous condition conducive to trip and falls. The two-inch lip of the slab is a dangerous condition.

[Place domino four on the jury rail.]

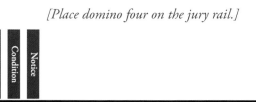

4. Domino Four: Notice of Condition

» The defendants have been in control of the premises for several years, and this type of condition is one that develops over time. The defendants conducted snow removal on the premises since they obtained the property and should have discovered this defect during the snow removal process or should have discovered it with reasonable inspections.

[Place domino five on the jury rail.]

5. Domino Five: The Fall Down

» The plaintiff, while entering the premises and looking at the signs posted in the window advertising a sale, tripped over the raised sidewalk slab and fell to the ground. The plaintiff immediately suffered an onset of neck pain. (Pain they had never before experienced)

[Place domino six on the jury rail.]

6. Domino Six: Immediate Onset of Pain

» The plaintiff immediately felt pain in her back and shoulder and a passerby called 911. The ambulance arrived and transported the plaintiff to the emergency room.

[Place domino seven on the jury rail.]

7. Domino Seven: Emergency Room

» The plaintiff is taken to the hospital complaining of back and shoulder pain. She is examined, x-rayed, and discharged home.

Place domino eight on the jury rail.

8. Domino Eight: Chiropractor

» The plaintiff begins treatment with a local chiropractor for her back pain. The chiropractor refers her to an orthopedist to examine her shoulder.

Place domino nine on the jury rail.

9. Domino Nine: Orthopedist

» The orthopedist examines the plaintiff and, after positive physical findings, refers her for MRIs of the back and shoulder. Her pain continues.

Place domino ten on the jury rail.

10. Domino Ten: MRI

» MRIs of the plaintiff's lumbar spine and shoulder are performed. The spine imaging reveals degenerative disc disease with a right-sided herniated disc superimposed on a bulge at L5-S1. The plaintiff's shoulder is positive for a partial rotator cuff tear. Physical therapy is prescribed.

Place domino eleven on the jury rail.

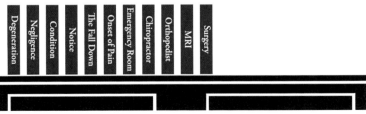

11. Domino Eleven: Surgery

» After physical therapy fails to help, the plaintiff undergoes three epidurals, and surgery is ultimately performed.

Place domino twelve on the jury rail.

12. Domino Twelve: Continued Pain

» The plaintiff continues to have limited range of motion and pain in her lumbar spine. Her shoulder has improved, but is still painful at the extremes of her ROM.

» Again, this is a great place to add the actual damages dominos sustained by your client.

Place domino thirteen on the jury rail.

13. Domino Thirteen: Today

» The plaintiff has experienced pain for the last four years following the accident until the present day.

Place domino fourteen on the jury rail.

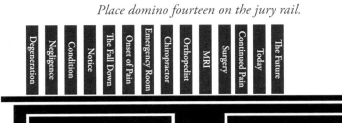

14. Domino Fourteen: The Future

» The injuries caused by this accident will not only last from the time of the accident but will also last into the future and probably worsen. The plaintiff has a life expectancy of thirty-two years. She may live longer or she may live shorter. This is an estimate the jury can utilize to wholly compensate the plaintiff.

34

DOMINO THEORY DEMONSTRATION THREE:
Proving Proximate Cause of Lost Wages

Money, it's a crime. Share it fairly but don't take a slice of my pie.

Roger Waters

I have also used the domino theory just to prove lost income. In a recent trial of mine, the defendants argued that my client got laid off and did not lose his job as a sewer maintenance supervisor because of the injuries he suffered from a head-on collision. However, when I received his employment file, it was clear that something had occurred around the time of the accident because prior to it his performance evaluations were stellar.

He received raises, promotions, and above-average marks in every category of his performance evaluations. In fact, in thirteen years he received twenty-six biannual reviews that were exemplary. The defense tried to claim that because of the economy, and not the accident, he was simply laid off. It did not help that his former boss testified during deposition that he was in fact laid off due to the economy and then came into court and reiterated that fact.

I thought it was too much of a coincidence that, following the accident, he began to have excessive absences, took six weeks off to recover from a shoulder surgery, and did not assist his coworkers in the hands-on physical aspect of the job. I also had to deal with a prior accident with intermittent neck pain. That case was handled by another lawyer, a few years before the case I was trying. In the case prior to mine, according to interrogatories so terribly drafted it is a miracle I was able to win the case at all, they claimed my client could no longer do anything. There was a laundry list of activities the prior lawyer claimed my client could no longer perform, including lifting, bending, squatting, kneeling, walking, running, working, and so on. Despite the previous lawyer leaving no room for anything to claim from the second accident, with regard to lost income, here is how I laid out the dominos.

DEMONSTRATING
PROXIMATE CAUSE OF LOST WAGES

[Place domino one on the jury rail.]

Neck Pain

1. Domino One: Intermittent Neck Pain

» There was evidence from prior interrogatories from an accident in 2006 that the plaintiff still suffered from intermittent neck pain. The plaintiff certified he had a bulging disc in his neck and that the intermittent neck pain was permanent and would continue indefinitely. He'd had very little treatment for the injury to his neck from that prior accident and ultimately had two herniated discs where the bulges were from this accident and received a cervical fusion surgery. So, just like dealing with degeneration in a typical soft-tissue injury, I had to deal with a prior accident and an admission of continued neck pain prior to this accident, despite a relatively minor prior injury to his neck.

This is why, when you answer interrogatories, you cannot throw the kitchen sink at the defense. The less serious injuries that resolve have to be given up. Claim only the serious injuries as permanent. As I placed the domino on the rail, I stated that we knew he had a prior injury to his neck, but it had occurred in 2006 and he had still received six stellar reviews following that accident. So although he was slightly injured, it had not affected his work performance.

[Place domino two on the jury rail.]

2. Domino Two: Twenty-Six Stellar Reviews

> Prior to this accident, the plaintiff had been working for thirteen years at his job at the sewage treatment plant. He received promotions, raises, and twenty-six biannual reviews of his work performance. They were stellar.

[Place domino three on the rail.]

3. Domino Three: Negligence

> But then the defendant is speeding and crosses the double yellow-line. He is negligent. By driving into oncoming traffic, above the posted speed limit, he did not act reasonably.

[Place domino four on the jury rail.]

4. Domino Four: Collision

» The cars collide as Mr. Raymond pulls out of the driveway. The airbag deploys, striking him in the face, and snapping his head back.

[Place domino five on the jury rail.]

5. Domino Five: Ambulance

» The ambulance arrives.

[Place domino six on the jury rail.]

6. Domino Six: Emergency Room

» The plaintiff is taken to the hospital complaining of neck and shoulder pain.

[Place domino seven on the jury rail.]

7. Domino Seven: Doctors

» The plaintiff begins treatment with his doctor.

[Place domino eight on the jury rail.]

8. Domino Eight: Chiropractor

» Pain continues and the plaintiff sees the chiropractor seventy times.

[Place domino nine on the jury rail.]

9. Domino Nine: MRI

» MRIs of the cervical spine and left shoulder are recommended and performed, revealing herniations at the levels where prior bulges were present.

[Place domino ten on the jury rail.]

10. Domino Ten: Epidurals

» The plaintiff is referred to pain management and receives three cervical epidurals.

[Place domino eleven on the jury rail.]

11. Domino Eleven: Family Leave Act

» Mr. Raymond takes six-weeks leave to undergo left-shoulder surgery.

[Place domino twelve on the jury rail.]

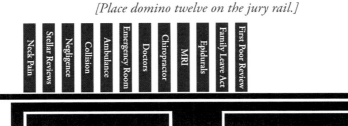

12. Domino Twelve: First Poor Review

» In July 2009, Mr. Raymond receives his first poor evaluation for excessive absences.

[Place domino thirteen on the jury rail.]

13. Domino Thirteen: Second Poor Review
» In February 2010, Mr. Raymond receives his second consecutive unsatisfactory work evaluation for continued unexcused absences.

[Place domino fourteen on the jury rail.]

14. Domino Fourteen: Laid Off
» Mr. Raymond is allegedly laid off in March, 2010, as a result of the economy. He goes on unemployment and loses $124,000 until he gets another job. He is replaced two weeks later by a new hire.

[Place domino fifteen on the jury rail.]

15. Domino Fifteen: Spine Specialist
» Surgery is performed.

[Place domino sixteen on the jury rail.]

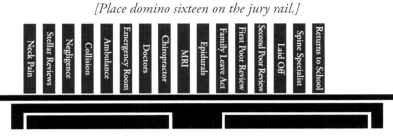

16. Domino Sixteen: Returns to School

» The plaintiff still has complaints four years following the accident and goes back to school to learn the computer business.

[Place domino seventeen on the jury rail.]

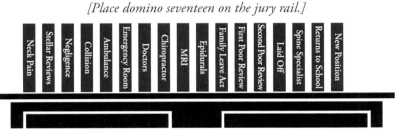

17. Domino Seventeen: New Position

» Mr. Raymond obtains a job at a computer company making significantly less than he was at his prior job.

[Place domino eighteen on the jury rail.]

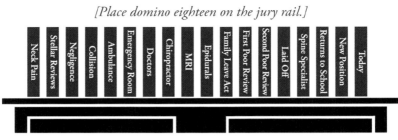

18. Domino Eighteen: Today

»And here we are today, four years after the accident. As you can see it is clear, despite his employer's and the defendant's argument, that the plaintiff's lost income was caused by the accident and not the economy.

The following is an excerpt from the closing argument in this case, where I used the domino theory to prove the defendant's negligence was a proximate cause of the accident, the injuries, and ultimately the plaintiff's lost income:

Now, you heard from Stan Smith. You didn't hear from an economist for the defense and say this is not true. It's completely true. It's completely probable and it's probably what's going to happen to him. He worked at OMI. If he had worked at OMI, where he had worked for fourteen years before this, he would have made, until he's sixty-seven years, $2,737,329 net. That's what he would have taken home if he continued to work there until 2043. But instead, he's—now goes back to

school, becomes a computer specialist who—the average computer specialist—this is based on US labor
statistics. This is not a made up number. He would
have made, until sixty-two—remember, he said well,
because he's disabled, he's only going work until sixty-
two. His loss of income, because he only would have
made $2 million at his prior job, now based on what
he will make now going forward, he will lose $718,000
over the course of his life. But I said to him—and this
was to be fair. But what if he does computers until he's
sixty-seven? But dollars in the future, these are not dollars now. If you're making $55,000 a year now, in 2043
that $55,000 is worth $82,000 because of inflation.
So, if you add five more years at $82,000—and that's
if he's probably making $82,000—it's $410,000. So,
I said, let's take off $410,000 and the loss of income
would be worth the same amount of time—and the
same amount of lifetime, would be only $308,000 less.
So, ladies and gentlemen, the questions that you guys
are going to have to answer are—let me give you a little
demonstration—is whether or not the negligence of
the defendant was a proximate cause of the damages
being his loss of income and his injuries and all that.

[Here is where I begin to place the dominos on the jury rail.]

Well, if you recall, he had intermittent neck pain in
March of 2006. That was according to those answers to
interrogatories from the prior accident. Before this accident, he had twenty-six stellar reviews from his job.
So, if this accident doesn't happen, these things just
go on. He's got intermittent neck pain. He's got those
twenty-six reviews, thirty-six, forty-six, fifty-six, sev-
enty-six, for the rest of his life. But then what happens

is, Juan Coburn is negligent. Juan Coburn is speeding in a residential section, Juan Coburn is crossing the double yellow-line unsafely, and a collision occurs. Mr. Raymond is taken by ambulance to the hospital. He starts seeing doctors. He gets three epidural injections. He goes to the chiropractor seventy times. He undergoes a new MRI that reveals two herniated discs. He also has an MRI of the left shoulder that reveals a tear of the rotator cuff. He goes out on Family Leave Act for six weeks. Receives shoulder surgery. Gets his first poor review on July 21, 2009. Excessive absences. Just four weeks after returning from his leave. February 2010, another bad review. He loses his job in May. He's laid off. Goes back to school and changes his career and then loses between $718,000 and $308,000. Continues to experience neck pain and receives neck surgery. And now here we are today.

I did win this trial and the jury did give the plaintiff a lost wage award, which I believe would have been impossible without the domino theory. I also got tagged for 49% negligence, which really upset me because there was no way he was even 1% negligent. Juries can break your heart. But with the domino theory your case will be tighter because you will be consciously connecting the dots and making the difficult principle of proximate cause easy to understand.

35

THE AGONY OF DEFEAT

Victory has a thousand fathers but defeat is an orphan.

President John F. Kennedy

You can't win 'em all. I have won trials I should have lost, lost trials I should have won, and everything in between. When I started writing this chapter, ironically, I had just taken a no cause verdict on a construction case. I am still hurting from that loss. It was the most difficult case I have ever tried.

I still proved proximate cause using the domino theory. The jury found my client 60 percent negligent and the defendant 40 percent negligent for the accident. New Jersey is a comparative negligence state. If we do not get at least 50 percent or more negligence on the defendant, we collect zero. But I do take some comfort in the fact that they found the defendant's negligence was the proximate cause of the accident and injuries. Proximate cause, as usual, was the most difficult element of the case to prove.

I can always find some solace in a loss if I lose five to one or can at least prove my case to one juror. In this case, I did prove the defendant negligent, and that his negligence was a proximate cause of the accident and injuries; unfortunately, my client's negligence outweighed that of the defendant. The jury deliberated for two days, and I thought I had them, but it was not to be. I lost seven to one on the allocation of negligence.

When I began writing this chapter, I had just taken a defense verdict. However, I started another trial back-to-back with that prior one and well, I just resumed writing after taking a plaintiff's verdict. So as you can see, moods, emotions, and other things can change rapidly when you are constantly on trial. You win some and you lose some.

It's a roller coaster ride. Do not be afraid of trying cases. We are trial lawyers and trying cases is what we do. I have a sign in my garage with a photo of Babe Ruth that says, "Don't let the fear of striking out get in the way of hitting a home run." You will never receive a large verdict without going to bat. You can only try your best, and if you are well prepared and you have a meritorious case, you will win. You must accept winning with the same emotion as when you lose. Believe me, a loss can be devastating, but all you can do is be the best you can be. Prepare and be yourself. This crazy roller coaster ride is worth every penny. You are a trial lawyer, part of one of the most noble professions in the world. You fight for the little guy, those injured by the negligence of others. I am so proud to be a plaintiff's trial lawyer and so should you be. I never would have changed the name of the American Trial Lawyers Association (ATLA) to the American Association for Justice (AAJ). I know in my heart I am one of the good guys. I fight for the people, not to pad my wallet. I love being a lawyer. I truly feel if we put our clients' interests before our own, as we should anyway, we can change the world one case at a time.

As for me, I am going to continue to fight insurance companies and try as many cases as I can, to try and change the deceptive practices they utilize everyday against the citizens of the United States. I am also going to continue to combat defense medical experts, expose them for what they are, fight for my clients' rights, and continue to strive to become the best attorney I can. You only live once.

APPENDIX

PROXIMATE CAUSE DEFINITIONS OR JURY INSTRUCTIONS BY STATE

Alabama

The proximate cause of an injury is that cause which, in a natural and probable sequence of events, and without intervention of any new or independent cause, produces the injury and without which such injury would not have occurred.[1]

Alaska

Negligence is a substantial factor in causing harm if:

(1) the harm would not have occurred without the negligence; and

(2) the negligence was important enough in causing the harm that a reasonable person would hold the negligent person responsible. The negligence cannot be a remote or trivial factor.[2]

Arizona

Before you can find any party [person] at fault, you must find that party's [person's] negligence was a cause of the plaintiff's injury.

Negligence causes an injury if it helps produce the injury, and if the injury would not have happened without the negligence. There may be more than one cause of an injury.[3]

---

1 Alabama Pattern Jury Instructions—Civil, § 33.00.

2 Alaska Civil Pattern Jury Instructions, § 03.07 "Substantial Factor."

3 Revised Arizona Jury Instructions (Civil), 5th Edition.

Arkansas

The law frequently uses the expression *proximate cause* with which you will not be familiar. When I use the expression proximate cause, I mean a cause which, in a natural and continuous sequence, produces damage and without which the damage would not have occurred.[4]

California

Causation: Substantial Factor

A substantial factor in causing harm is a factor that a reasonable person would consider to have contributed to the harm. It must be more than a remote or trivial factor. It does not have to be the only cause of the harm.

[Conduct is not a substantial factor in causing harm if the same harm would have occurred without that conduct.][5]

Colorado

9:18 Cause When Only One Cause is Alleged—Defined

The word "cause" as used in these instructions means an act or failure to act which in natural and probable sequence produced the claimed injury. It is a cause without which the claimed injury would not have happened.[6]

9:21 Cause—Foreseeability Limitation

The negligence, if any, of the defendant, (name), is not a cause of any (injuries) (damages) (losses) to the plaintiff, (name), unless injury to a person in the plaintiff's situation was a reasonably foreseeable result of that negligence. The specific injury need not have been foreseeable. It is enough if a reasonably careful person, under the same or similar circumstances, would

---

4 Arkansas Model Jury Instructions, § 501.

5 California Civil Jury Instructions, § 430 "Causation: Substantial Factor."

6 Colorado Jury Instructions, Civil, 4th Edition (2015), § 9.18.

have anticipated that injury to a person in the plaintiff's situation might result from the defendant's conduct.[7]

Connecticut
Negligence is a proximate cause of an injury if it was a substantial factor in bringing the (injury/harm) about.[8]

Delaware
A party's negligence, by itself, is not enough to impose legal responsibility on that party. Something more is needed: the party's negligence must be shown by a preponderance of the evidence to be a proximate cause of the [accident/injury].

Proximate cause is a cause that directly produces the harm, and but for the harm would not have occurred. A proximate cause brings about, or helps to bring about, the [accident/injury], and it must have been necessary to the result.[9]

Florida
Negligence is a legal cause of [loss] [injury] [or] [damage] if it directly and in natural and continuous sequence produces or contributes substantially to producing such [loss] [injury] [or] [damage], so that it can reasonably be said that, but for the negligence, the [loss] [injury] [or] [damage] would not have occurred.[10]

Georgia
Proximate cause is that which, in the natural and continuous sequence, unbroken by other causes, produces an event and without which the event would not have occurred. Proximate cause

---

7 Colorado Jury Instructions, Civil, 4th Edition (2015), § 9.21.

8 Connecticut Civil Jury Instructions, § 3.1-3 "Proximate Cause—Definition."

9 Pattern Jury Instructions for Civil Practice in the Superior Court of the State of Delaware (2000), § 21.1 "Proximate Cause."

10 Florida Standard Jury Instructions—Civil Cases, § 401.12 "Legal Cause."

is that which is nearest in the order of responsible causes, as distinguished from remote, that which stands last in causation, not necessarily in time or place, but in causal relation.[11]

Hawaii

An act or omission is a legal cause of an injury/damage if it was a substantial factor in bringing about the injury/damage.

One or more substantial factors such as the conduct of more than one person may operate separately or together to cause an injury or damage. In such a case, each may be a legal cause of the injury/damage.[12]

Idaho

When I use the expression *proximate cause*, I mean a cause which, in a natural or probable sequence, produced the complained injury, loss, or damage, and but for that cause the damage would not have occurred. It need not be the only cause. It is sufficient if it is a substantial factor in bringing about the injury, loss, or damage. It is not a proximate cause if the injury, loss, or damage would have occurred anyway.[13]

Illinois

When I use the expression *proximate cause*, I mean a cause that in the natural or ordinary course of events produced the plaintiff's injury. It need not be the only cause, nor the last or nearest cause. It is sufficient if it combines with another cause, resulting in injury.[14]

---

11 Council of Superior Court Judges of Georgia. *Georgia Suggested Pattern Jury Instructions*, Vol. 1, *Civil Cases*, 5th ed. (Athens: University of Georgia, 2007), 60.200 (Proximate Cause) O.C.G.A. §§51-12-3, 51-12-8, 51-12-9.

12 Hawaii Civil Jury Instructions (1999), § 7.1 "Legal Cause."

13 Idaho Civil Jury Instructions, § 2.30.1 "Proximate Cause—'But For' Test."

14 Illinois Pattern Jury Instructions—Civil, § 15.01.

Indiana

A person's conduct is legally responsible for causing [an injury] if: The [injury] would not have occurred without the conduct, and The [injury] was a natural, probable, and foreseeable result of the conduct.[15]

Iowa

In 2009, the Iowa Supreme Court adopted the Restatement (Third) of Torts formula for determining causation.[16] The Restatement (Third) retains the concept of factual cause but does away with the doctrine of proximate cause in favor of a "scope of liability" doctrine.

> 1. Factual cause: "Conduct is a factual cause of harm when the harm would not have occurred absent the conduct."[17]

> 2. Scope of liability: "An actor's liability is limited to those physical harms that result from the risks that made the actor's conduct tortious. . . . An actor is not liable for physical harm when the tortious aspect of the actor's conduct was of a type that does not generally increase the risk of that harm."[18]

Kansas

Kansas appellate courts have consistently defined *proximate cause* as "that cause which in a natural and continuous sequence, unbroken by an efficient intervening cause, produces

---

15 IJA Indiana Model Jury Instructions, § 301 "Responsible Cause."

16 *See Thompson v. Kaczinski*, 774 N.W.2d 829, 836–839 (Iowa 2009).

17 Restatement (Third) of Torts: Liab. for Physical Harm § 26 (Proposed Final Draft No. 1, 2005); accord Iowa Uniform Civil Jury Instruction 700.3.

18 *Royal Indem. Co. v. Factory Mut. Ins.* Co., 786 N.W.2d 839, 850 (Iowa 2010) (quoting Restatement (Third) of Torts: Liab. for Physical Harm §§ 29–30 (Proposed Final Draft No. 1, 2005)).

the injury and without which the injury would not have occurred, the injury being the natural and probable consequence
of the wrongful act."[19]

Kentucky
The actor's negligent conduct is a legal cause of harm to another
if his conduct is a substantial factor in bringing about the harm,
and there is no rule of law relieving the actor from liability because
of the manner in which his negligence has resulted in the harm.[20]

Louisiana
"Duty/Risk" Instruction—Emphasis on Proximate Cause
The second major issue you have to decide is whether the defendant did actually act in a manner below the standard which
I've told you applies to his conduct. To find the defendant's
conduct substandard, you would have to conclude that as an
ordinarily prudent person under all the circumstances sur-
rounding his conduct, the defendant should have reasonably
foreseen some injury such as the plaintiff suffered, and you
would also have to conclude that he failed to exercise reasonable care to avoid the injury.[21]

Maine
An injury or damage is legally caused by an act, or by a failure to
act, whenever the act or failure to act played a substantial part in
bringing about or actually causing the injury or damage and the
injury or damage was either a direct result or a reasonably foreseeable consequence of the act or failure to act.

19 *Idbeis v. Wichita Surgical Specialists,* 285 Kan. 485, 499, 173 P.3d 642 (2007).

20 *Deutsch v. Shein* 597 S.W.2d 141 (Ken. 1980) (Restatement Torts (Second) Sec. 431).

21 H. Alston Johnson III. *Civil Jury Instructions*, 3rd ed. Louisiana Civil Law
Treatise Series, Vol. 18 (Thomson West, 2016), § 3:15.

When Causation is a Serious Issue

An injury or damage is a direct result of an act or failure to act when the act or failure to act starts an event or chain of events that inevitably leads to the injury or damage. This is an objective test: Did the act or failure to act start events which made the injury or damage inevitable, regardless of whether the injury or damage could have been foreseen?

An injury or damage is a reasonably foreseeable consequence of an act or failure to act when that act or failure to act creates a risk which might reasonably be expected to result in the injury or damage in question, even though the exact person injured or the exact nature of the injury need not, itself, be foreseeable. This is a subjective test: Could the injury or damage reasonably have been foreseen to result from the risk created by the act or failure to act?

The term legal cause rather than proximate cause is used in the instruction because some jury studies have found that jurors may confuse the term *proximate* with *approximate*.[22]

Maryland

For the plaintiff to recover damages, the defendant's negligence must be a cause of the plaintiff's injury. [There may be more than one cause of an injury, that is, several negligent acts may work together. Each person whose negligent act is a cause of an injury is responsible.][23]

Massachusetts

A person's conduct or failure to act may be negligent and yet that person may not be liable for negligence. Thus, if the jury finds the defendant has breached a duty of care, it must next consider whether the defendant's breach effectively caused the plaintiff's injuries. In other words, the jury must consider whether the

22 Donald G. Alexander. *Maine Jury Instruction Manual* (LexisNexis, 2013), § 7-80.

23 Maryland Civil Pattern Jury Instructions, § 19:10 "Causation."

defendant's breach was the *proximate cause* of the plaintiff's injuries. The proximate cause analysis focuses on whether the cause is a *substantial factor* in bringing about the plaintiff's injuries.[24]

For a negligent act or omission to be a proximate cause of a personal injury, it must be established that the personal injury would not have occurred "but for" the negligent act or omission.[25]

If the plaintiff's injury would have occurred in any event, regardless of the defendant's negligence, the defendant's negligence cannot be said to have been a proximate cause of that injury. Although, there may be more than one proximate cause of a plaintiff's injury.

Whether negligent conduct is the proximate cause of an injury ultimately depends on whether the injury to the plaintiff was a *foreseeable result* of the defendant's negligent conduct.[26] Such conduct may be a proximate cause of injury if, in the natural and continuous sequence, it produces the injury.[27]

It must also be established that the chain of causation between the defendant's negligence and the plaintiff's injury was not broken by some new or *intervening* cause. Most often, an intervening cause is an independent negligent or criminal act of a third party, occurring after the negligent act or omission of the defendant and before a subsequent injury to the plaintiff. An intervening cause will be sufficient to break the chain of causation only if the commission of such an act was not *reasonably foreseeable* by the defendant at the time of his negligent act or omission. If the third

---

24 *O'Connor v. Raymark Industries, Inc.*, 401 Mass. 586 (1988) and *Wallace v. Ludwig*, 292 Mass. 251, 257 (1935).

25 *Teasdale v. Beacon Oil Co.*, 266 Mass. 25 (Mass. 1929).

26 *Commonwealth v. Angelo Todesca Corp.*, 446 Mass. 128, 141 (2006), quoting *Kent v. Commonwealth*, 437 Mass. 312, 320 (2002).

27 Id., citing *Commonwealth v. Osachuk*, 43 Mass. App. Ct. 71, 73 (1997), quoting *Commonwealth v. Rhoades*, 379 Mass. 810, 825 (1980).

party's actions were reasonably foreseeable at the time of the accident, the chain of causation is not broken.[28]

Michigan

When I use the words *proximate cause* I mean first that the negligent conduct must have been a cause of the plaintiff's injury, and second, that the plaintiff's injury must have been a type that is the natural and probable result of the negligent conduct.[29]

Minnesota

A *direct cause* is a cause that had a substantial part in bringing about the *(collision)(accident)(event)(harm)(injury).*[30]

Mississippi

In order for (name of defendant] to be legally responsible for [name of plaintiff]'s damages, [name of defendant]'s negligence must have (1) actually caused [name of plaintiff]'s damages and (2) a reasonable [person/business/corporation] would have anticipated that some damages would occur as a result of [name of defendant]'s negligence.

In order to be a legal cause, [name of defendant]'s negligence must have been a substantial factor in causing [name of plaintiff]'s damages. If [name of plaintiff] would have suffered damages even if [name of defendant] had not been negligent, then [name of defendant]'s negligence was not a substantial factor in causing [name of plaintiff]'s damages.[31]

---

28 *O'Connor v. Raymark Industries, Inc.*, 401 Mass. 586 (1988) and *Wallace v. Ludwig*, 292 Mass. 251, 257 (1935).

29 Michigan Model Civil Jury Instructions, § 15.01.

30 Minnesota District Judges Association Committee on Jury Instruction Guides—Civil. *Minnesota Jury Instruction Guides—Civil*, 6th ed. Minnesota Practice Series, Vol. 4 (Thomson West, 2014), § 27.10.

31 Mississippi Model Jury Instructions—Civil, §§ 15:2–15:4.

Missouri
Single Negligent Act Submitted
Your verdict must be for plaintiff if you believe:

First, the defendant violated the traffic signal, and

Second, the defendant was thereby negligent, and

Third, as a direct result of such negligence, the plaintiff sustained damage.[32]

Montana
The defendant's conduct is a cause of the (injury/death/damage) if, in a natural and continuous sequence, it helped produce it and if the (injury/death/damage) would not have occurred without it.[33]

Nebraska
In a negligence action, the jury usually should be instructed on proximate cause. It should be told that the proximate cause is the efficient, and not a remote, cause.[34]

A proximate cause is a cause that produces a result in a natural and continuous sequence, and without which the result would not have occurred.[35]

32 Missouri Supreme Court Committee on Jury Instructions. *Missouri Approved Jury Instructions (MAI), Civil,* 7th ed. (Thomson West, 2016), §§ 17.01, 17.02, 19.01.

33 Sarah A. Dixon. "Montana's Law of Causation: History, Analysis and a Proposal for Change," *Montana Law Review* 57, no. 2 (Summer 1996).

34 Nebraska Supreme Court Committees on Civil and Criminal Procedure. *Nebraska Jury Instructions—Civil & Criminal,* 2016–2017 ed. Nebraska Practice Series, Vol. 1 (Thomson West, 2016), § 3.41 "Proximate Cause."

35 Ibid.

Nevada

A proximate cause of injury, damage, loss or harm is a cause which, in natural and continuous sequence, produces the injury, damage, loss, or harm, and without which the injury, damage, loss, or harm, would not have occurred.[36]

New Hampshire

Failure to exercise reasonable care amounts to legal fault if you find that such failure was a legal cause of the accident and injury. When is negligence the legal cause of harm? When the negligent conduct is a substantial factor in bringing about the harm, and if the harm would not have occurred without that conduct.

On the other hand, if the negligent conduct is not a substantial factor in bringing about the harm, it cannot be the basis for a finding of legal harm.

In determining whether the defendant's conduct was a legal cause of the plaintiff's injury, you need not find that the defendants conduct was the sole cause of the injury. You need only find that it was a substantial factor in bringing about the injury, even though other factors may also have contributed to cause the injury.[37]

New Jersey

By proximate cause, I refer to a cause that in a natural and continuous sequence produces the accident/incident/event and resulting injury/loss/harm and without which the resulting accident/incident/event or injury/loss/harm would not have occurred. A person who is negligent is held responsible for any accident/incident/event or injury/loss/harm that results in the ordinary course of events from his/her/its negligence. This means that you must first find that the resulting accident/incident/event

36 State Bar of Nevada. *Nevada Jury Instructions—Civil*, (Las Vegas: State Bar of Nevada, 2011), § 4.04.

37 Daniel C. Pope. *New Hampshire Civil Jury Instructions*, (LexisNexis, 2016), § 6.1.

or injury/loss/harm to *[name of plaintiff or other party]* would not have occurred but for the negligent conduct of *[name of defendant or other party]*. Second, you must find that *[name of plaintiff or defendant]* negligent conduct was a substantial factor in bringing about the resulting accident or injury/loss/harm. By substantial, I mean that the cause is not remote, trivial or inconsequential.

If you find that *[name of defendant or other party]'s* negligence was a cause of the accident/incident/event and that such negligence was a substantial factor in bringing about the injury/loss/harm, then you should find that *[name of defendant or other party]* was a proximate cause of *[name of plaintiff]'s* injury/loss/harm.[38]

New Mexico

An [act] [or] [omission] [or] [condition] is a "cause" of [injury] [harm] [other] if [,unbroken by an independent or intervening cause,] it contributes to bringing about the [injury][harm][other] [, and if injury would not have occurred without it]. It need not be the only explanation for the [injury][harm][other], nor the reason that is nearest in time or place. It is sufficient if it occurs in combination with some other cause to produce the result. To be a "cause," the [act] [or][omission][or][condition] nonetheless, must be reasonably connected as a significant link to the [injury] [harm].[39]

New York

An act or omission is regarded as a cause of an injury [in bifurcated trial, substitute: accident or occurrence] if it was a substantial factor in bringing about the injury [in bifurcated trial, substitute: accident or occurrence], that is, if it had such an effect in producing the injury [in bifurcated trial, substitute: accident or occurrence] that reasonable people would regard it as a cause of

---

38 New Jersey Model Jury Charges (Civil) 6.11 "Proximate Cause" (August 1999).
39 NM UJI 13-305.

the injury [in bifurcated trial, substitute: accident or occurrence]. [The remainder of the charge should only be provided where there is evidence of comparative fault or concurrent causes.] There may be more than one cause of an injury [in bifurcated trial, substitute: accident or occurrence], but to be substantial, it cannot be slight or trivial. You may, however, decide that a cause is substantial even if you assign a relatively small percentage to it.[40]

North Carolina
Proximate cause is a cause which in natural and continuous sequence, unbroken by any new and independent cause, produced the plaintiff's injuries, and without which the injuries would not have occurred, and one from which a person of ordinary prudence could have reasonably foreseen that such a result, or some similar injurious result, was probable under the facts as they existed.[41]

North Dakota
A proximate cause is a cause which, in natural and continuous sequence, produces the injury, and without which, the injury would not have occurred. It is a cause which had a substantial part in bringing about the injury either immediately or through events which follow one another.

[There may be more than one proximate cause of the injury. The fault of two or more persons may contribute to cause the injury, and in such case, each person's fault is regarded as a proximate cause.][42]

40 New York Pattern Jury Instruction, § 2:70 "Proximate Cause—In General."

41 John M. Strong and Lawyers Cooperative Publishing. *Strong's North Carolina Index* (St. Paul: West Group) Negligence, § 8.

42 State Bar Association of North Dakota. *North Dakota Pattern Jury Instructions, Civil*, Vol. 2 (State Bar Association of North Dakota, 2012) § 2.15.

Ohio

The exact language of a jury instruction is within the discretion of the trial court.[43] The following definition was held as acceptable by the Appellate Court of Ohio:

> "Proximate cause exists where an act or failure to act, in a natural and continuous sequence, directly produced the injury and without which it would not have occurred.
>
> "There may be more than one proximate cause. The fact that some other cause combined with the negligence of a defendant in producing an injury does not relieve him/her from liability, unless it is shown such other cause would have produced the injury independently of defendant's negligence."[44]

Oklahoma

Direct cause means a cause which in a natural and continuous sequence produces injury and without which the injury would not have happened. For negligence to be a direct cause it is necessary that some injury to [the property of] a person in [plaintiff's] situation must have been a reasonably foreseeable result of negligence.[45]

Oregon

The law assumes that all persons have obeyed the law and have been free from [fault/negligence]. The mere fact alone that an accident happened or that a person was injured is not sufficient of itself to prove negligence. It is, however, a circumstance that may be considered along with other evidence.

---

43 *Youssef v. Parr, Inc.*, (1990), 69 Ohio App.3d 679, 690, 591 N.E.2d 762, citing *State v. Scott*, (1987), 41 Ohio App.3d 313, 535 N.E.2d 379 paragraph three of syllabus.

44 *Musil v. Truesdell*, 2010-Ohio-1579.

45 Oklahoma Uniform Jury Instructions, § 9.8 "Direct Cause."

To recover, the plaintiff must prove two things by a preponderance of the evidence: (1) that the defendant was [at fault/negligent] in at least one of the ways claimed in the plaintiff's complaint; and (2) that the defendant's [fault / negligence] was a cause of damage to the plaintiff.

[Similarly, for the defendant to prevail on the defendant's claim that the plaintiff was (at fault/negligent), the defendant must prove two things by a preponderance of evidence: (1) that the plaintiff was (at fault/negligent) in at least one of the ways claimed in the defendant's answer; and (2) that the plaintiff's (fault/negligence) was a cause of damage to the defendant.][46]

Pennsylvania

In order for [name of plaintiff] to recover in this case, [name of defendant]'s [negligent] [grossly negligent] [reckless] conduct must have been a factual cause in bringing about harm. Conduct is a factual cause of harm when the harm would not have occurred absent the conduct. To be a factual cause, the conduct must have been an actual, real factor in causing the harm, even if the result is unusual or unexpected. A factual cause cannot be an imaginary or fanciful factor having no connection or only an insignificant connection with the harm.

To be a factual cause, [name of defendant]'s conduct need not be the only factual cause. The fact that some other causes concur with [name of defendant]'s negligence in producing an injury does not relieve [name of defendant] from liability as long as [his] [her] own negligence is a factual cause of the injury.[47]

---

46 Oregon Jury Instructions for Civil Cases, UCJI No. 20.01 "Fault/Negligence and Causation."

47 Civil Instructions Subcommittee of the Pennsylvania Supreme Court Committee for Proposed Standard Jury Instructions. *Pennsylvania Suggested Standard Civil Jury Instructions*, 4th Ed. (Mechanicsburg: PBI Press, 2015), § 13.20.

Rhode Island

An injury or damage is proximately caused by an act, or a failure to act, whenever it appears from the evidence in the case that the act or omission played a substantial part in bringing about or causing the injury or damage, and that the injury or damage was either a direct result or a reasonably probable consequence of the act or omission. The plaintiff must prove that the injury or damage would not have occurred but for the defendants' acts, and the defendants' acts must be shown to have been a direct, rather than a remote, cause of the injury.[48]

South Carolina

Proximate cause is something that produces a natural chain of events which, in the end, brings about the injury. It is the direct cause of the injury.

To prove that the defendant's negligence proximately caused the plaintiff's injury, the plaintiff must first prove causation in fact. This is proven by showing that the injury would not have occurred but for the defendant's negligence.

The plaintiff must also prove legal cause. Legal cause is proven by showing that the injury was foreseeable. This means that the injury occurred as a natural and probable consequence of the defendant's negligence. The plaintiff must prove that some injury from the defendant's negligence was foreseeable, but does not have to prove that the particular injury that occurred was foreseeable. However, the defendant cannot be held responsible for things which could not be expected to happen. Proximate cause does not mean the only cause. The defendant's act can be a proximate cause of the plaintiff's injury if it was at least one of the direct, concurring causes of the injury.[49]

48 *Morris v. Rhode Island Hospital*, 2014 WL 3107296 (D.R.I. 2014).

49 *Small v. Pioneer Mach., Inc.*, 329 S.C. 448, 494 S.E.2d 835 (Ct. App. 1997). South Carolina Civil Jury Charges, pp. 57-58 available at http://www.judicial.state.sc.us/juryCharges/CivilChargesJune2013.pdf

South Dakota

When the expression *proximate cause* is used, it means an immediate cause of any injury, which, in natural or probable sequence, produces the injury complained of. Without the proximate cause, the injury would not occur. The proximate cause need not be the only cause, nor the last or nearest cause. It is sufficient if it concurs with some other cause acting at the same time, which in combination with it causes the injury.

For proximate cause to exist, you must find that the harm suffered was a foreseeable consequence of the act complained of.[50]

Tennessee

A legal cause of any injury is a cause which, in natural and continuous sequence, produces an injury, and without which the injury would not have occurred.[51]

Texas

That cause which, in a natural and continuous sequence, produces an event, and without which cause such event would not have occurred. In order to be a proximate cause, the act or omission complained of must be such that a person using ordinary care would have foreseen that the event, or some similar event, might reasonably result therefrom. There may be more than one proximate cause of an event. Proximate cause consists of two parts, both of which must be proved. The parts are (1) cause in fact and (2) foreseeability.[52] *Cause in fact* is an essential element of every tort recognized in *Texas. Crum & Forster, Inc. v. Monsanto Co.*, 887 S.W.2d 103, 130 (Tex. App.—Texarkana 1994, no writ). Cause in fact means that the act or omission complained of was

50 *Wuest ex rel. Carter v. McKennan Hospital*, 619 N.W.2d 682, 689 (S.D. 2000).

51 Tennessee Pattern Jury Instructions TPI—Civil, § 3.20 "Definition of Legal Cause."

52 *Doe v. Boys Clubs of Greater Dallas, Inc.*, 907 S.W.2d 472, 477 (Tex. 1995).

a substantial factor in bringing about the injury or damages, and without the act or omission, no harm would have occurred to the plaintiff.[53] The issue of foreseeability only arises once it is established that the defendant's conduct was one of the causes in fact of the plaintiff's injury. Foreseeability requires a court to determine a question of legal policy—whether the defendant should be responsible for the plaintiff's injuries.[54] The inclusion of the foreseeability element in proximate causation analysis represents judicial recognition that "[a]t some point in the causal chain, the defendant's conduct or product may be too remotely connected with the plaintiff's injury to constitute legal causation."[55]

Utah

I've instructed you before that fault is a wrongful act or failure to act. You must also determine whether a person's fault caused the harm. As used in the law, the word "cause" has a special meaning, and you must use the meaning whenever you apply the word. "Cause" means that:

> The person's act or failure to act produced the harm directly or set in motion events that produced the harm and in a natural and continuous sequence; and

> The persons act or failure to act could be foreseen by a reasonable person to produce a harm of the same general nature.[56]

Vermont

You must decide if the [accident and/or plaintiff's injuries] was actually caused by [something name of defendant did or failed to do].

---

53 *Doe v. Boys Clubs of Greater Dallas*, Inc., 907 S.W.2d 472, 477 (Tex. 1995).

54 *City of Gladewater v. Pike*, 727 S.W.2d 514, 518 (Tex. 1987).

55 *Union Pump Company v. Allbritton*, 898 S.W.2d 773, 775 (Tex. 1995).

56 (Model Utah Jury Instructions 3:13, 3:14, 3:15 and utcourts.gov).

Alternate (1): That is to say, if [name of defendant] had not been negligent, then [name of plaintiff] would not have been hurt.

Alternate (2): That is, without the negligence would [name of plaintiff] been injured?

Alternate (3): That is, without the negligence would the accident have happened?

Alternate (4): In other words, had [name of defendant] not [made left turn, set off firecracker, pushed the lady onto the train car, etc] the [accident/injury] would not have happened.[57]

Virginia

The proximate cause of an event is that act or omission that, in natural and continuous sequence, unbroken by an efficient intervening cause, produces the event, and without which that event would not have occurred.

The proximate cause of an event is a cause that, in natural and continuous sequence, unbroken by any efficient intervening cause, produces the event, and without which the event would not have occurred. It is an act or omission that immediately causes or fails to prevent the event; an act or omission occurring or concurring with another act, without which the event would not have occurred; provided such event could reasonably have been anticipated by a prudent man in the light of attendant circumstances.[58]

---

57 Vermont Civil Jury Instructions, § 4.0 "Proximate Cause."

58 Virginia Practice Series Jury Instruction, § 11:9 "Proximate Cause."

Washington

The term *proximate cause* means a cause in which a direct sequence [unbroken by any superseding cause] produces the [injury] [event] complained of and without which such [injury/event] would not have happened.[59]

West Virginia

The proximate cause of an event is that cause which in actual sequence unbroken by any independent cause produces an event, and without which the event would not have occurred. It is not necessary that the jury find that a particular defendant's negligence, if any, was the only cause of Plaintiff's injury. It is only necessary that you find by a preponderance of the evidence that such negligence was a proximate cause of the injury.[60]

Wisconsin

No set words are essential or exclusive in defining such cause. It may be defined as the efficient cause, that which acts first and produces the injury, as a natural and probable result, under such circumstances that he who is responsible for such cause, as a person of ordinary intelligence and prudence, ought reasonably to foresee that a personal injury to another may probably follow from such person's conduct. It is not, necessarily, the immediate, near, or nearest, cause, but the one that acts first, whether immediate to the injury or such injury be reached by setting other causes in motion, each in order being started, naturally, by the one that precedes it, and altogether constituting a complete chain or succession of events, so united to each other by a close causal

---

59 Washington State Supreme Court Committee on Jury Instructions. *Washington Pattern Jury Instructions—Civil*, Washington Practice Series, (2013), § WPI 15.01 "Proximate Cause—Definition."

60 *Reynolds v. City Hospital*, Inc. 207 W.Va. 101, 108 (W.Va. 2000).

connection as to form a natural whole, reaching from the first or producing cause to the final result.[61]

Wyoming

An injury or damage is caused by an act, or a failure to act, whenever it appears from the evidence in the case that the act or omission played a substantial part in bringing about the injury or damage.[62]

Proximate cause is explained as "the accident or injury must be the natural and probable consequence of the act of negligence."[63] The ultimate test of proximate cause is foreseeability of injury.[64] In order to qualify as a legal cause, the conduct must be a substantial factor in bringing about the plaintiff's injuries.[65]

---

61 *Deisenrieter v. Kraus-Merkel Malting Co.*, 72 N.W. 735, 738 (Wis. 1897) See also 4A Wis. Pl. & Pr. Forms § 33:121 (5th ed.).

62 *Turcq v. Shanahan*, 950 P.2d 47, 1997.

63 *Bettencourt v. Pride Well Service, Inc.*, 735 P.2d 722, 726 (Wyo.1987); followed in, Natural Gas Processing Co. v. Hull, 886 P.2d 1181, 1186 (Wyo.1994); *Lynch v. Norton Const., Inc.*, 861 P.2d 1095, 1099 (Wyo.1993).

64 *Stephenson v. Pacific Power & Light Co.*, 779 P.2d 1169, 1178 (Wyo.1989); *McClellan v. Tottenhoff*, 666 P.2d 408, 414 (Wyo.1983).

65 Natural Gas Processing Co., 886 P.2d at 1186; Stephenson, 779 P.2d at 1178.

OTHER LEGAL DEFINITIONS
OF PROXIMATE CAUSE

West's Encyclopedia of American law, 2nd Edition
Proximate Cause

An act from which an injury results as a natural, direct, uninterrupted consequence and without which the injury would not have occurred.

Proximate cause is the primary cause of an injury. It is not necessarily the closest cause in time or space nor the first event that sets in motion a sequence of events leading to an injury. Proximate cause produces particular, foreseeable consequences without the intervention of any independent or unforeseeable cause. It is also known as legal cause.

To help determine the proximate cause of an injury in Negligence or other tort cases, courts have devised the "but for" or *sine qua non* rule, which considers whether the injury would not have occurred but for the defendant's negligent act. A finding that an injury would not have occurred but for a defendant's act establishes that the particular act or omission is the proximate cause of the harm, but it does not necessarily establish liability since a variety of other factors can come into play in tort actions.

Some jurisdictions apply the *substantial factor* formula to determine proximate cause. This rule considers whether the defendant's conduct was a substantial factor in producing the harm. If the act was a substantial factor in bringing about the damage, then the defendant will be held liable unless she can raise a sufficient defense to rebut the claims.[66]

66 Jeffrey Lehman and Shirelle Phelps. *West's Encyclopedia of American Law*, 2nd ed. (Detroit: Thomson/Gale, 2008).

The People's Law Dictionary
Proximate Cause

A happening which results in an event, particularly injury due to negligence or an intentional wrongful act. In order to prevail (win) in a lawsuit for damages due to negligence or some other wrong, it is essential to claim (plead) proximate cause in the complaint and to prove in trial that the negligent act of the defendant was the proximate cause (and not some other reason) of the damages to the plaintiff (person filing the lawsuit). Sometimes there is an intervening cause which comes between the original negligence of the defendant and the injured plaintiff, which will either reduce the amount of responsibility or, if this intervening cause is the substantial reason for the injury, then the defendant will not be liable at all. In criminal law, the defendant's act must have been the proximate cause of the death of a victim to prove murder or manslaughter.[67]

Nolo's Plain-English Law Dictionary
Legal Cause

A cause that produces a direct effect, and without which the effect would not have occurred. (See also: direct and proximate cause)[68]

67 *The People's Law Dictionary*, "Proximate Cause," accessed October 19, 2016, http://dictionary.law.com/Default.aspx?selected=1669#ixzz3jMMv6sNr

68 *Nolo's Plain English Law Dictionary*, "Legal Cause," accessed October 19, 2016, http://www.nolo.com/dictionary/legal-cause-term.html

ACKNOWLEDGMENTS

I wrote this book because I believe that if you work hard, get creative, and do your own thing you can change the world. You can make a difference. I would like to thank all of the great lawyers I am blessed to have worked with or learned from during my career in addition to those I have already mentioned. From New Jersey: Michael Maggiano, Michael Ferrara, Don Caminiti, Chris Placitella, Ken Andres, Drew Britcher, Abbott Brown, Amos Gern, Tim Barnes, Gerry Baker, Tom Comer, Tom Vesper, Eric Kahn, Bruce Nagel, Kevin Costello, Bruce Stern, Michael Donohue, Norman Hobbie, Norberto Garcia, Jae Lee, Chip Walden, Marc Saperstein, Gary Salomon, Sam Davis, Jim and Arthur Lynch, Pat Mangan, Kate Reilly, Dan Rosner, John Gorman, Nick Leonardis, Keith Roberts, Charlie Gormally, and Mark Managin to name a few.

Seth Belsen, who I interned for at the Public Defender's Office, was instrumental in showing me how to be myself in a courtroom and arguing from my heart with passion. I watched how he handled himself in court and it was impressive. Instead of citing law, and presenting the case in a robotic fashion, as most attorneys do, he would tell the judge at a bail hearing, "This guy is a great guy, he deserves another chance. I know he will return for his trial, he is innocent and wants his day in court." Time after time, I would watch the judge release the defendant on his own recognizance. Seth has remained a great friend and mentor to me ever since I began my career as a trial lawyer. Seth is also a big Eagles and Phillies fan and when I received my New Jersey Law Journal Hall of Fame Award for receiving the highest verdict in the State in 2013 for a product liability case, he gave me his prized Mike Schmidt autographed bat. It hangs on my wall next to my Derek Jeter autographed bat.

I have attended many seminars all over the United States and some of the speakers truly touched my soul and made me want to be a better lawyer. I cannot thank them all enough. John Romano, Jim Lees, Gerry Spence, David Ball, Rick Friedman, Dorothy Clay Sims, Mark Lanier, Ron Motley and so many others. I hope I can offer some of the same enthusiasm to all of you, as they all gave to me.

ABOUT THE AUTHOR

Edward P. Capozzi is a plaintiff's personal injury trial attorney in the State of New Jersey and a partner at Brach Eichler LLC. He is certified by the Supreme Court of New Jersey as a civil trial attorney for his expertise at trial in civil matters. After a long career as a musician and performer, he left the stage and entered the courtroom where he is known for his fierce cross-examinations of medical witnesses and artistic presentations of his cases. Mr. Capozzi has had at least one, and as many as three, of the top twenty verdicts and settlements in the State of New Jersey for five consecutive years. In 2014, he received the *New Jersey Law Journal*'s Hall of Fame Award for the highest verdict in the state for a products liability case. He has been named to Best Attorneys in America, the Top 1 percent of Attorneys in America, and has been selected to Super Lawyers and Top Attorneys in NJ every year since 2012. Mr. Capozzi specializes in trucking, auto, and premises liability matters, including elevator incidents. In 2015, he received the fifth largest verdict or settlement in the State. He has represented seriously injured clients in New Jersey, New York, Pennsylvania, North Carolina, Michigan, West Virginia, Florida, Massachusetts, Virginia, Maryland, and Delaware.

Mr. Capozzi is a vice president of the New Jersey Association for Justice (NJAJ), a Leader's Forum member of the American Association for Justice (AAJ), an advocate member of the American Board of Trial Advocates (ABOTA), a member of the Association of Plaintiff Interstate Trucking Lawyers of America

(APITLA), the American Bar Association (ABA), and the New Jersey State Bar Association (NJSBA). He regularly lectures throughout the United States on trucking, cross-examination of defense experts, and proving proximate cause at trial. He is married to his wife, Mariana, a school teacher, and has four children: Alex, James, Olivia, and Thomas. He is a collector of historical, sports, and music related memorabilia and an avid sports fan of the Yankees, Rangers, Jets, and Knicks.